International Workshop on Computational Terminology

(COMPUTERM 2002)

Held at COLING 2002

Taipei, Taiwan
31 August 2002

ISBN: 978-1-63439-677-6

Printed from e-media with permission by:

Curran Associates, Inc.
57 Morehouse Lane
Red Hook, NY 12571

CURRAN ASSOCIATES INC. proceedings.com

Some format issues inherent in the e-media version may also appear in this print version.

Printed by Curran Associates, Inc. (2015)

Association for Computational Linguistics
209 N. Eighth Street
Stroudsburg, Pennsylvania 18360

Phone: 1-570-476-8006
Fax: 1-570-476-0860

acl@aclweb.org

Additional copies of this publication are available from:

Curran Associates, Inc.
57 Morehouse Lane
Red Hook, NY 12571 USA
Phone: 845-758-0400
Fax: 845-758-2634
Email: curran@proceedings.com
Web: www.proceedings.com

Disambiguating Noun Compounds with Latent Semantic Indexing

Alan M. Buckeridge and **Richard F. E. Sutcliffe**
Department of Computer Science and Information Systems,
University of Limerick, Limerick, Ireland
{Alan.Buckeridge, Richard.Sutcliffe}@ul.ie

Abstract

Technical terms in text often appear as noun compounds, a frequently occurring yet highly ambiguous construction whose interpretation relies on extra-syntactic information. Several statistical methods for disambiguating compounds have been reported in the literature, often with quite impressive results. However, a striking feature of all these approaches is that they rely on the existence of previously seen unambiguous compounds, meaning they are prone to the problem of sparse data. This difficulty has been overcome somewhat through the use of hand-crafted knowledge resources to collect statistics on "concepts" rather than noun tokens, but domain-independence has been sacrificed by doing so. We report here on work investigating the application of Latent Semantic Indexing to provide a robust domain-independent source of the extra-syntactic knowledge necessary for noun compound disambiguation.

1 Introduction

Noun compounds are a frequently encountered construction in natural language processing (NLP), consisting of a sequence of two or more nouns which together function syntactically as a noun. In English, compounds consisting of two nouns are predominantly right-headed. However, compound construction is recursive and both the modifier and the head can themselves be compounds, resulting in structural ambiguities. Consider the following pair of noun compounds:

1. (a) (*cantilever* (*swing wing*))
   (b) ((*information retrieval*) *experiment*)

Both compounds consist of the same parts-of-speech, yet the structures differ: (1a) is right-branching, while (1b) is left-branching.

Phrase structure grammar rules for noun compounds are often similar in form to $\overline{N} \rightarrow \overline{N}\,\overline{N}$ (Lauer, 1995). This rule is applied once to two-word noun compounds, and recursively in the case of longer compounds; therefore the syntax of compounds longer than two words is underconstrained by grammar, resulting in a syntactic ambiguity which grows exponentially with the length of the compound.

Besides causing problems for syntactic parsers, the ambiguities inherent in these structures pose difficulties for NLP systems which attempt to analyse the underlying semantic relationships present in compound technical terms. Often, the first step in such analyses is to decompose terms into nested modifier-head pairs (Barker, 1998). However, such a decomposition is non-trivial for the case of compounds consisting of three or more nouns due to the structural ambiguity of these constructions.

The identification of modifier-head pairs in compounds also has applications within the field of information retrieval (IR). Several studies have shown that extracting modifier-head pairs from text and including these as compound indexing terms can improve recall and precision (Evans and Zhai, 1996; Pohlmann and Kraaij, 1997; Strzalkowski and Vauthey, 1992). Identification of these noun modifier relationships is also important for terminology translation. However, obtaining correct modifier-head pairs is once again hampered by "the notorious ambiguity of nominal compounds" (Strzalkowski and Vauthey, 1992, p.107).

To summarise, the syntactic disambiguation of noun compounds is important for several NLP applications; however, disambiguation is difficult because attachments within compounds are not syntactically governed. Clearly, then, this lack of syntactic constraints forces us to consider the use of extra-syntactic factors in the process of disambiguation. The work reported here describes an approach for automatically deriving a syntactical analysis of noun compounds by adapting Latent Semantic Indexing, a well-established IR technique, to supply this extra-syntactic information.

2 Previous Work

The majority of corpus statistical approaches to compound disambiguation use a variation of what Lauer (1995) refers to as the *adjacency algorithm*. This algorithm was originally proposed by Marcus (1980), and essentially operates by comparing the acceptability of immediately adjacent noun pairs. Specifically, given a sequence of three nouns *n1 n2 n3*, if (*n2 n3*) is a more acceptable constituent than (*n1 n2*), then build (*n1* (*n2 n3*)); else build ((*n1 n2*) *n3*).

There remains the question of how "acceptability" is to be determined computationally. Several researchers (e.g., (Barker, 1998; Evans and Zhai, 1996; Pohlmann and Kraaij, 1997; Pustejovsky et al., 1993; Strzalkowski and Vauthey, 1992)) collect statistics on the occurrence frequency of structurally unambiguous two-noun compounds to inform the analysis of the ambiguous compound. For example, given the compound "computer data bases", the structure (*computer* (*data bases*)) would be preferred if (*data bases*) occurred more frequently than (*computer data*) in the corpus. However, by assuming that sufficient examples of subcomponents exist in the training corpus, all the above approaches risk falling foul of the *sparse data problem*. Most noun-noun compounds are rare, and statistics based on such infrequent events may lead to an unreliable estimation of the acceptability of particular modifier-head pairs.

The work of Resnik (1993) goes some way towards alleviating this problem. Rather than collecting statistics on individual words, he instead counts co-occurrences of *concepts* (as represented by WordNet synsets). He uses these statistics to derive a measure, motivated by information theory, called *selectional association* (see Resnik (1993) for full details). "Acceptability" in the adjacency algorithm is then measured in terms of the selectional association between a modifier and head. Selectional associations were calculated by training on approximately 15,000 noun-noun compounds from the *Wall Street Journal* corpus in the Penn Treebank. Of a sample of 156 three-noun compounds drawn from the corpus, Resnik's method achieved 72.6% disambiguation accuracy.

Lauer (1995) similarly generalises from individual nouns to semantic classes or concepts; however, his classes are derived from semantic categories in Roget's Thesaurus. Similar to the approaches discussed above, Lauer extracts a training set of approximately 35,000 unambiguous noun-noun modifier-head compounds to estimate the degree of association between Roget categories. He calls this measure *conceptual association*, and uses this to calculate the acceptability of noun pairs for the disambiguation of three-noun compounds. However, his approach differs from most others in that he does not use the adjacency algorithm, instead using a *dependency algorithm* which operates as follows: Given a three-noun compound *n1 n2 n3*, if (*n1 n3*) is more acceptable than (*n1 n2*), then build (*n1* (*n2 n3*)); else build ((*n1 n2*) *n3*).

Lauer tested both the dependency and adjacency algorithms on a set of 244 three-noun compounds extracted from Grolier's Encyclopedia and found that the dependency algorithm consistently outperformed the adjacency algorithm, achieving a maximum of 81% accuracy on the task. Overall, he found that estimating the parameters of his probabilistic model based on the distribution of concepts rather than that of individual nouns resulted in superior performance, thus providing further evidence of the effectiveness of conceptual association in noun compound disambiguation.

All these approaches rely on a variation of finding subconstituents elsewhere in the corpus and using these to decide how the longer, ambiguous compounds are structured. However, there is always the possibility that these systems might encounter modifier-head pairs in testing which never occurred in training, forcing the system to "back off" to some default strategy. This problem is alleviated somewhat in the work of Resnik and Lauer where statistics are collected on pairs of *concepts* rather than pairs of noun tokens. However, the methods of

Resnik and Lauer both depend on hand-crafted knowledge sources; the applicability of their approaches is therefore limited by the coverage of these resources. Thus their methods would almost certainly perform less well when applied to more technical domains where much of the vocabulary used would not be available in either WordNet or Roget's Thesaurus. Knowledge sources such as these would have to be manually augmented each time the system was ported to a new domain. Therefore, it would be preferable to have a method of measuring conceptual associations which is less domain-dependent and which does not rely on the presence of unambiguous subconstituents in training; we investigated whether Latent Semantic Indexing might satisfy these requirements.

3 Latent Semantic Indexing

Latent Semantic Indexing (LSI) is a variant of the vector-space approach to information retrieval. It takes as input a collection of documents, from which it constructs an $m \times n$ word-document matrix A; cell a_{ij} of the matrix denotes the frequency with which term i occurs in document j. At the core of LSI is *singular value decomposition* (SVD), a mathematical technique closely related to eigenvector decomposition and factor analysis. SVD factors the matrix A into the product of three matrices: $A = U\Sigma V^T$. U and V contain the left and right singular vectors of A, respectively, while Σ is a diagonal matrix containing the singular values of A in descending order. By retaining only the k largest singular values[1] and setting the remaining smaller ones to zero, a new diagonal matrix Σ_k is obtained; then the product of $U\Sigma_k V^T$ is the $m \times n$ matrix A_k which is only approximately equal to A. This truncated SVD re-represents the word-document relationships in A using only the axes of greatest variation, in effect compressing and smoothing the data in A. It is this compression step which is said to capture important regularities in the patterns of word co-occurrences while ignoring smaller variations that may be due to idiosyncrasies in the word usage of individual documents. The result of condensing the matrix in this way is that words which occur in similar documents will be represented by similar vectors, even if these words never actually co-occur in the same document. Thus it is claimed that LSI captures deeper associative relationships than mere word-word co-occurrences. See Berry et al. (1995) and Deerwester et al. (1990) for more thorough discussions of SVD and its application to information retrieval.

Because word vectors are originally based on their distribution of occurrence across documents, each vector can be interpreted as a summary of a word's contextual usage; words are thus similar to the extent that they occur in similar contexts. Of interest for our purposes is the fact that a measure of the similarity or association between pairs of words can be calculated geometrically, typically by computing the cosine of the angle between word vectors. Any two words, which may or may not occur adjacently in text, can be compared in this way; this frees us from the restriction of relying on unambiguous subconstituents in training to inform the analysis of ambiguous compounds in testing.

There is a growing body of literature indicating that distributional information of the kind captured by LSI plays an important role in various aspects of human cognition. For the work reported here, the most interesting aspect of distributional information is its purported ability to model conceptual categorisation. Several studies (Burgess and Lund, 1999; Laham, 1997; Landauer et al., 1998; Levy and Bullinaria, 2001) have shown that similarity between concepts can be measured quite successfully using simple vectors of contextual usage; results show that the performance of such systems correlates well with that of humans on the same tasks. These results are all the more impressive when we consider that such systems use no hand-coded semantic knowledge; the conceptual representations are derived automatically from training corpora.

Noun compound disambiguation appears to be an NLP application for which such measures of conceptual association would be useful. Both the adjacency and dependency algorithms described above in Section 2 rely on some measure of the "acceptability" of pairs of nouns to disambiguate noun compounds. Techniques such as LSI offer a simple, robust, and domain-

[1] The optimal value of k may only be determined empirically, and will depend on the particular application.

Noun Compound	Branching
((Ami Pro) document)	Left
(volunteer (rescue workers))	Right
(tourist (exchange rates))	Right
((cluster analysis) procedure)	Left
((data base) subcommittee)	Left
(Windows (Control Panel))	Right

Table 1: Some example noun compounds taken from our test set. Each row shows an example of a manually bracketed compound, along with its branching direction.

independent way in which concepts and the associations between them can be represented. In the next section, we describe an experiment exploring the efficacy of LSI's conceptual representations in disambiguating noun compounds.

4 LSI and Noun Compound Disambiguation

4.1 Method

4.1.1 Materials

We used four corpora in our study: The *Lotus Ami Pro Word Processor for Windows User's Guide Release 3*, a software manual (AmiPro); document abstracts in library science (CISI); document abstracts on aeronautics (CRAN); and articles from Time magazine (Time). We first ran the LSI software on the corpora to create the word-by-document matrices. The software also subsequently performed singular value decomposition on the resulting matrices. Stop-words were not excluded, as previous experience had shown that doing so degraded performance slightly.

We used Brill's (1994) tagger to identify three-noun sequences in each of the corpora. Tagging was imperfect, and sequences which were not true three-noun compounds were discarded. The remaining noun compounds were bracketed manually and constituted test sets for each corpus; some examples are shown in Table 1. Table 2 summarises the datasets used in our study.

4.1.2 Procedure

Both the adjacency and dependency models were investigated (see Section 2). Recall that the adjacency algorithm operates by comparing the acceptability of the subcomponents (*n1 n2*) and (*n2 n3*), whereas the dependency algorithm compares the acceptability of (*n1 n2*) and (*n1 n3*). "Acceptability" in our approach was measured by calculating the cosine of the angle between each pair of word vectors. The cosine ranges from -1.0 to 1.0; a higher cosine indicated a stronger association between each word in a pair. In the case of a tie, a left branching analysis was preferred, as the literature suggests that this is the more common structure (Lauer, 1995; Resnik, 1993). Thus a default strategy of always guessing a left branching analysis served as the baseline in this study. Each of the corpora contained terms not covered by WordNet or Roget's; thus it was not possible to use the techniques of Resnik (1993) and Lauer (1995) as baselines.

As we could not tell beforehand what the optimal value of k would be (see Section 3 above), we used a range of factor values. The values used ranged from 2 to the total number of documents in each collection. For each factor value, we obtained the percentage accuracy of both the adjacency and dependency models.

4.2 Results and Discussion

The results of the experiment are summarised in Table 3 and Figure 1. In most cases the performance rises quickly as the number of SVD factors used increases, and then tends to level off. The best performance was 84% for the AmiPro collection, obtained using the adjacency algorithm and 280 SVD factors. As the task involved choosing the best binary bracketing for a noun compound, we would expect an accuracy of 50% by chance. These results compare favourably with those of Resnik (1993) and Lauer (1995) (73% and 81%, respectively), but as their studies were conducted on different corpora, it would be imprudent to make direct comparisons at this stage. Results for the other collections were less impressive—however, above-baseline performances were obtained in each case.

Substantial differences in the performances of the adjacency and dependency algorithms were only observed for the AmiPro collection, suggesting that the superior performance of the dependency algorithm in Lauer's (1995) study was largely corpus-dependent. This is reinforced by the considerably superior performance of the

Collection Name	AmiPro	CISI	CRAN	Time
Number of Documents	704	1,460	1,400	425
Number of Tokens	138,091	187,696	217,035	252,808
Mean Tokens per Type	46.3	18.7	26.2	11.5
Number of test compounds	307	235	223	214

Table 2: Characteristics of the datasets.

Name	AmiPro	CISI	CRAN	Time
Baseline	58%	63%	74%	48%
Adjacency	84% (280)	73% (800)	75% (700)	62% (370)
Dependency	70% (200)	70% (1100)	75% (600)	62% (240)

Table 3: Percentage disambiguation accuracy on each collection. The Baseline row shows the accuracy of always choosing a left-branching analysis. Highest accuracies for the Adjacency and Dependency algorithms are shown, with the corresponding number of SVD factors in parentheses.

adjacency algorithm on the AmiPro data set.

Another interesting finding was that there were more right-branching (52%) than left-branching (48%) compounds in the Time collection. This contrasts with previous studies which discuss the predominance of left-branching compounds, and suggests that the choice for the default branching must be corpus-dependent (see Barker (1998) for similar findings).

There also appears to be a positive relationship between performance and the token-type ratio. The number of tokens per type in the AmiPro collection was 46.3; the worst performance was found for the Time collection, which had only 11.5 tokens per type. There are at least two possible explanations for this relationship between performance and token-type ratio: First, there were more samples of each word type in the AmiPro collection—this may have helped LSI construct vectors which were more representative of each word's contextual usage, thus leading to the superior performance on the AmiPro compounds.

Second, LSI constructs a single vector for each token—if a particular token is polysemous in text then its vector will be a "noisy" amalgamation of its senses, a factor often contributing to poor performance. However, due to the controlled language and vocabulary used in the software manual domain, few if any of the words in the AmiPro collection are used to convey more than one sense; once again, this may have resulted in "cleaner", more accurate vectors leading to the superior disambiguation performance on the AmiPro compounds.

These points lead us to the tentative suggestion that our approach appears most suitable for technical writing such as software manuals. As usual, however, this is a matter for future investigation.

5 Conclusions and Future Research

In this study, we extended LSI beyond its usual remit by adopting it as a measure of conceptual association for noun compound disambiguation. The results reported here are encouraging, the highest accuracy of 84% on the AmiPro collection indicating the potential of our approach. However, poorer performance was obtained for the other collections indicating that there is much room for improvement. We therefore intend to pursue our investigation of the utility of applying vector-based measures of semantic similarity to the problem of syntactic disambiguation. An attractive feature of this approach for the processing of terminology is that it requires no manually constructed knowledge sources, meaning that it does not suffer the same coverage limitations as the methods of Lauer (1995) and Resnik (1993). In principle, our approach can be applied to any domain.

Another attractive feature is that it does not rely on counts of unambiguous subconstituents in training. This means that it can be applied to novel compounds for which no subcompounds exist in training, something which would not be

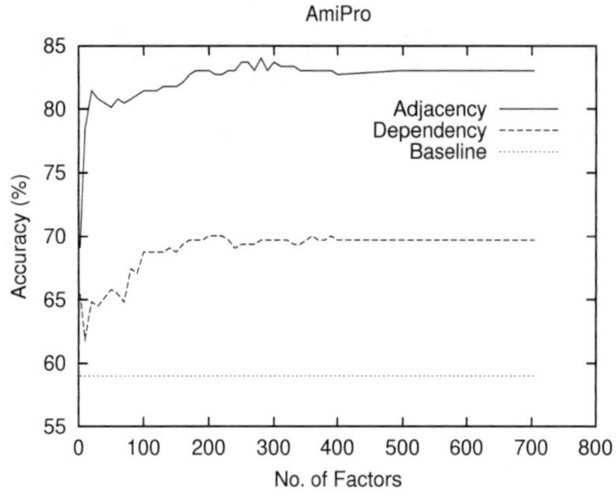

(a) AmiPro

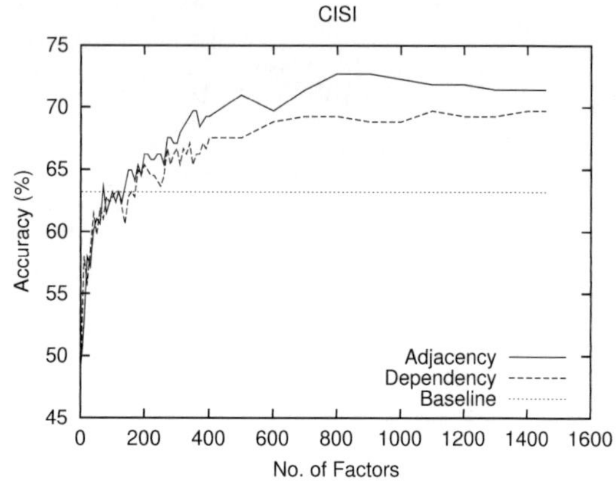

(b) CISI

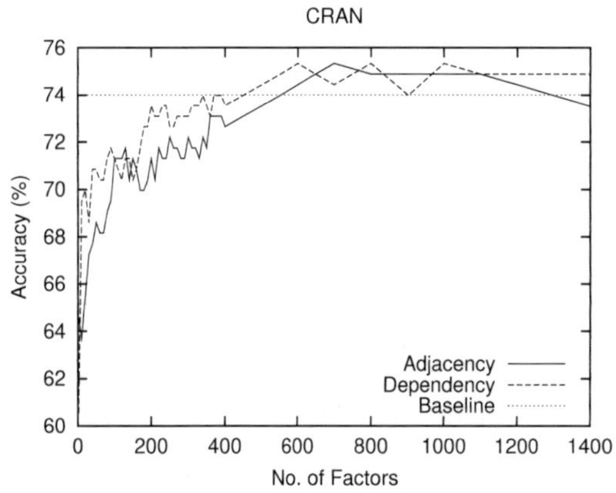

(c) CRAN

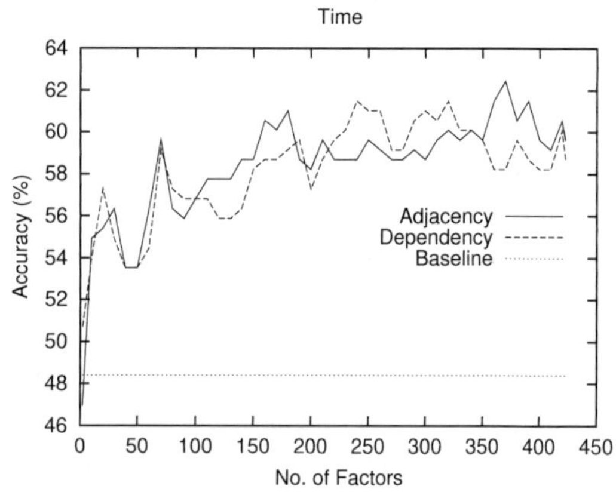

(d) Time

Figure 1: Results of an experiment investigating noun compound disambiguation using LSI. Each figure shows percentage disambiguation accuracy of the *adjacency* and *dependency* models for a range of SVD factors. The percentage of left-branching compounds in each test set, which served as the baseline in our study, is also shown for comparison.

possible for the statistical techniques outlined in Section 2. Our next step will thus be to investigate the efficacy of our approach on novel compounds.

We are currently examining the use of other techniques for deriving vector-based measures of conceptual association; preliminary investigations using a "sliding window" method (Burgess and Lund, 1999; Levy and Bullinaria, 2001) to disambiguate compounds from the AmiPro corpus show results even better than those reported here. Present work involves setting various parameters (e.g., window size, similarity metric, weighting method) to study their effect on performance. We are continuing to test both the adjacency and dependency algorithms on this corpus, and have consistently found better performance using the former.

Future work will involve continuing to test the technique in other domains; we also intend training on larger and more diverse corpora. Furthermore, we plan to investigate other examples of syntactic ambiguity, such as prepositional phrase attachment. Such structures pose many problems for traditional NLP systems, but may prove amenable to the techniques discussed in this paper.

6 Acknowledgements

Our thanks go to Pat Hickey of ECE, University of Limerick, for technical assistance; and to two anonymous reviewers for helpful comments.

References

K. Barker. 1998. A trainable bracketer for noun modifiers. In *Proceedings of the Twelfth Canadian Conference on Artificial Intelligence*, pages 196–210, Vancouver.

M. W. Berry, S. T. Dumais, and T. A. Letsche. 1995. Computational methods for intelligent information access. In *Proceedings of Supercomputing '95*, San Diego, CA.

E. Brill. 1994. Some advances in transformation-based part of speech tagging. In *Proceedings of the 12th National Conference on Artificial Intelligence (AAAI-94)*.

C. Burgess and K. Lund. 1999. The dynamics of meaning in memory. In E. Dietrich and A. Markman, editors, *Cognitive Dynamics: Conceptual and Representational Change in Humans and Machines*, pages 17–56. Lawrence Erlbaum Associates Inc., Hillsdale, NJ.

S. Deerwester, S. T. Dumais, G. W. Furnas, T. K. Landauer, and R. Harshman. 1990. Indexing by latent semantic analysis. *Journal of the American Society for Information Science*, 41:391–407.

D. A. Evans and C. Zhai. 1996. Noun-phrase analysis in unrestricted text for information retrieval. In *Proceedings of the 34th Annual Meeting of the Association for Computational Linguistics*, pages 17–24, Santa-Cruz, CA, June.

D. Laham. 1997. Latent Semantic Analysis approaches to categorization. In *Proceedings of the 19th Annual Conference of the Cognitive Science Society*, page 979. Erlbaum.

T. K. Landauer, P. W. Foltz, and D. Laham. 1998. Introduction to Latent Semantic Analysis. *Discourse Processes*, 25:259–284.

M. Lauer. 1995. *Designing Statistical Language Learners: Experiments on Noun Compounds.* Ph.D. thesis, Macquarie University, Sydney, Australia.

J. P. Levy and J. A. Bullinaria. 2001. Learning lexical properties from word usage patterns: Which context words should be used? In *Proceedings of the Sixth Neural Computation and Psychology Workshop*, pages 273–282. London: Springer.

M. Marcus. 1980. *A Theory of Syntactic Recognition for Natural Language.* MIT Press, Cambridge, MA.

R. Pohlmann and W. Kraaij. 1997. The effect of syntactic phrase indexing on retrieval performance for Dutch texts. In *Proceedings of RIAO '97*, pages 176–187, Montréal, June.

J. Pustejovsky, S. Bergler, and P. Anick. 1993. Lexical semantic techniques for corpus analysis. *Computational Linguistics*, 19(2):331–358.

P. S. Resnik. 1993. *Selection and Information: A Class-Based Approach to Lexical Relationships.* Ph.D. thesis, University of Pennsylvania.

T. Strzalkowski and B. Vauthey. 1992. Information retrieval using robust natural language processing. In *Proceedings of the 30th Annual Meeting of the Association for Computational Linguistics*, pages 104–111, Newark, Delaware, USA.

An Intelligent Terminology Database as a Pre-processor for Statistical Machine Translation

Michael Carl and **Philippe Langlais**
RALI / DIRO / Université de Montréal
Montréal (Québec), Canada
email:{carl;felipe}@iro.umontreal.ca

Abstract

In a recent study Langlais (Langlais, 2002) has shown that the output of a Statistical Machine Translation (SMT) system deteriorates significantly the more the new text differs from the text the system has been trained on. Langlais shows that bilingual terminological databases are resources that can be taken into account to boost the performance of the statistical engine. This paper extends the notion of 'terminological databases' to an Intelligent Terminological Database (ITDB) capable to detect and reduce terms and their variants and to re-generate the authorized target language terms. The paper discusses the aims and the architecture of the ITDB and evaluates its integration with a SMT system.

1 Introduction

SMT mainly became known to the linguistic community as a result of the seminal work of Brown et al. (1993). Since then, many researchers have invested effort into designing better models than the ones proposed in the aforementioned article and several new exciting ways have been proposed to attack the problem[1].

In a recent paper Langlais (2002) investigated how a statistical engine behaves when translating a very domain-specific text far different from the corpus used to train both the translation and language models used by the engine. Langlais measured a significant drop in performances mainly due to `out-of-vocabulary words` and specific terminology that the models handle poorly. He then proposed to overcome the problem by opening the engine to available (non statistical) terminological resources. This contrasts to a previous approach of (Brown et al., 1993) who develop a statistical model of a bilingual dictionary which is then integrated with training text. Both authors find, however, that terminological databases are resources that boost the performance of a statistical translation engine.

With the possibility to introduce prior knowledge resources into SMT it becomes also interesting to explore their linguistic modeling and to investigate the adaptability of SMT systems to different domains. In this paper, we investigate a possibility to integrate an Intelligent Terminological Database (ITDB) as a pre-processor for an SMT system. This ITDB has the main advantage over simple lists of terms which were used in (Langlais, 2002) as to recognized terminological variants.

Terminological variants are cumbersome in every MT System as they introduce ambiguities which have to be resolved during translation. On the one hand side it is unrealistic and undesirable to list every possible variant in a terminological lexicon. On the other hand, the appropriate target language term has to be generated by the MT engine. In order to overcome this gap, the ITDB follows an abductive approach: a number of possible variants are abduced in a pre-processing step from a list of authorized term translations. The variants and the authorized terms are stored in a database which is consulted at run-time of the tool[2]. The idea being that variants in the source text can thus be traced back to their authorized form and translated properly.

The ITDB is an enhanced version of a ter-

[1] See for instance (Och and Ney, 2000) for a comparison of several translation models.

[2] Variants and Terms are stored in an under-specified format such that the size of the database increases much more slowly than the number of abduced variants. For a more detailed discussion see (Carl et al., 2002).

minology tool described in (Carl et al., 2002) which was adapted and modified here for the bilingual application.

The first part of this paper outlines the aims and architecture of the ITDB. The second part discusses a number of experiments. In section 2, we give an idea of the variants we want to tackle in the ITDB and discuss a number of terminological variants found in an aligned text. Section 3 presents the architecture of the ITDB and section 4 underpins its basic assumptions. In section 5 we show how variants are abduced from a bilingual terminology and sections 6 and 7 report on two experiments.

2 Aim of the ITDB

We have examined an English-French sentence aligned bilingual text form a military domain. The text — which we refer to as SNIPER2 — is a manuals on sniper training and deployment that was used in a previous study (Macklovitch, 1995, cf. section 6).

The text consists of 391 English-French aligned sentences. We have focused on the following phenomena of term variation:

2.1 Variation by Omission

A number of omission variants can be distinguished. The examples (1b,2b) show omission variations for French. In (1b) the expansion pour armes is not specified while in (2b) the type of the lunette is under-specified. Following (Jacquemin, 1996, p. 425), these variants can be said to be in a generic/specific relation.

(1a) *general purpose weapons oil* ↔ huile polyvalente pour armes
(1b) *general purpose weapons oil* ↔ huile polyvalente
(2a) *Unertl telescopic sight* ↔ lunette de tir Unertl
(2b) *Unertl telescopic sight* ↔ lunette Unertl

2.2 Variation by Insertion

Variants by insertion are complementary to omission variants. While in the French term (3b) a new head word tireur is introduced the English term is modified by the additional participle *supported*. In (4b), the English term is permuted and function words are inserted.

(3a) *prone position* ↔ position couché
(3b) *prone supported position* ↔ position du tireur couché
(4a) *rifle butt* ↔ crosse du fusil
(4b) *butt of a rifle* ↔ crosse du fusil

2.3 Synonyms

In addition to insertion and omission, terms also appear as synonyms. As Hamond and Nazarenko (Hamon and Nazarenko, 2001) notice, synonyms may appear in the head and/or in the expansion of a compound. As these different variation processes overlap it becomes particularly difficult to identify the intended meaning. Consider, for instance, the two term-cluster (5a-e) and (6a-e). The terms on the left-hand side in (5a) and (5b) show English variants in their head nouns *telescope* and *scope* while the French variants on the right-hand side in (6a) and (6b) have different expansions tir and visée. There is an English omission variant in (6c) which is translated into a full-form French term and a number of French omission variants (5c,d,e 6d,e). Here it becomes particularly ambiguous and confusing to know whether the full-form authorized translation of French lunette is *spotting telescope* or *telescopic sight.*

(5a) *spotting telescope* ↔ lunette d'observation
(5b) *spotting scope* ↔ lunette d'observation
(5c) *spotting telescope* ↔ lunette
(5d) *telescope* ↔ lunette
(5e) *scope* ↔ lunette

(6a) *telescopic sight* ↔ lunette de visée
(6b) *telescopic sight* ↔ lunette de tir
(6c) *sight* ↔ lunette de tir
(6d) *telescopic sight* ↔ lunette
(6e) *sight* ↔ lunette

Synonyms and omission variants may thus appear simultaneously, multiplying the 'noise' in translations and aligned texts. It is, however, clear, that one would not like to store all these variants in a bilingual terminology.

3 Architecture of the ITDB

In order to recognize variants of terms and their translations, we have adopted and modified a monolingual terminology tool described in (Carl et al., 2002). The monolingual terminology tool

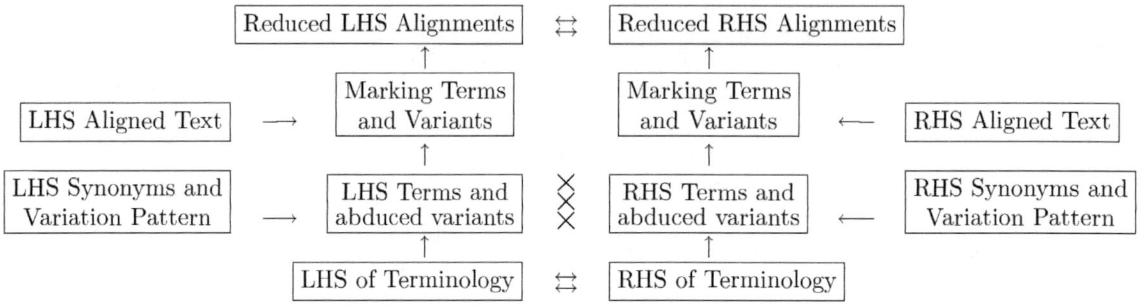

Figure 1: Components of the ITDB

and the ITDB integrate a rule-based formalism KURD and the example-based translation system EDGAR. The modified architecture of the bilingual terminology tool is shown in figure 1. It consists of two symmetrical language sides, a left-hand side (LHS, i.e. English) and a right-hand side (RHS, i.e. French). The architecture in figure 1 is designed to evaluate the performance of the ITDB. A runtime version of the ITDB is shown in figure 3 and discussed in section 7. In this section we describe the different parts of the evaluation architecture.

The ITDB assumes a bilingual terminology (cf. bottom in figure 1). This terminology is either provided by a terminologist or may be automatically acquired. In a study reported in section 6 we use a small bilingual terminology which was manually extracted from the SNIPER2 text. The bilingual terminology contains unambiguous term translations, indicated by the symbol $\leftrightarrow$.

A limited number of variants are generated through the process of "abduction" (discussed below) independently from each language side of a term. Abduction is performed by the rule-based formalism KURD which takes as its input a set of terms, a set of synonyms and a set of variation pattern (see figure 1). The abduced variants are stored in a database together with the original terms and each variant is linked to their authorized forms[3]. Abduction produces $m-to-n$ translations equivalences as indicated by the symbol $\times$.

A bilingual aligned text can now be matched against the database to mark terms and variants in the text as shown in the upper part in figure 1. We use the example-based translation system EDGAR which marks matched sequences of words in the text as variant or term according to the status of the matched database entry. To evaluate coverage and precision of the ITDB (cf. section 6), the marked sequences are reduced to a generic label which are counted and compared in LHS and RHS. In the runtime architecture (cf. figure 3), authorized target language forms of source language terms and their variants are re-generated as discussed in section 7.

4 An Abductive Approach

ITDB recognizes variants of terms by abduction. According to Streiter (Streiter, 2001), abductive reasoning creates hypothesis which are not logically implied by the premises. Unlike deductive reasoning, abduction is not always correct in all reasoning steps. However, abductive reasoning should be "plausible" in a context and yield correct results in the vast majority. Where deductive inference stops in front of gaps, abduction creates new hypothesis which allow to bridge the gap and continue the inference. As an illustration for abductive reasoning, Streiter gives the following example

> "Imagine, you ordered a product and a week later you received a parcel. Using abduction you might assume that this is what you ordered. In order to come to this conclusion you induce from single experiences $\exists(x,y)\ order(x,y) \wedge receive(x,y)$ a hypothesis $\forall(x,y)\ order(x,y) \rightarrow receive(x,y)$ and instantiate x and y with "I" and "product", so that you (safely) assume that you receive your

[3] cf. (Carl et al., 2002) for a more detailed description of this process.

(7)	*focusing ring*	↔	bague de mise au point
(8)	*eyepiece locking ring*	↔	bague de verrouillage de l'oculaire
(9)	*rearward movement*	↔	mouvement arrière

(7_{LHS_0})	*focusing (ring;buckle;collar;light;pneumatic;ripening; ...)*
(7_{RHS_0})	(bague;anneau;aggraver;bouche;boucle; ...) de mise au point
(7_{RHS_1})	bague;anneau;aggraver;bouche;boucle ...
(9_{LHS_0})	*(rearward;recompense;remunerate;pay;compensate) (movement;transport;traffic;trade;...)*
(9_{RHS_0})	(mouvement;émouvoir;transport;trafic;...) (arrière;fond;derrière;sévère;queue; ...)
(9_{RHS_2})	(mouvement;émouvoir;transport;trafic;...) x y (arrière;fond;derrière;sévère;queue; ...)

Figure 2: Abduction of Term Variants

product. "

Essentially, in Streiter's example, from the co-occurrence of two single experiences is inferred an implication containing a universal quantifier in the hypothesis. Abduction consists in re-instantiating the generated hypothesis by appropriate events to draw the desired conclusion.

Mooney (Mooney, 2000) examines the relation between abduction and induction. Although precise definitions of abduction and induction are still somewhat controversial, he finds:

> "In abduction, the hypothesis is a specific set of assumptions that explain the observations of a particular case; while in induction, the hypothesis is a general theory that explains the observations across a number of cases." (Mooney, 2000, p.183)

Mooney applies abductive learning for theory refinement. Theory refinement is the task to make an existing imperfect domain theory consistent with a set of data. For him, abduction is primary useful in generalizing a theory to cover more positive examples. For each individual positive example that is not derivable from the current theory, abduction is applied to determine a set of assumptions that would allow it to be proven.

In a similar way the ITDB detects and reduces terminological inconsistencies. The underlaying assumption in ITDB is that each term in the LHS of an alignment (or in a the source text) has also a translation in the RHS (or in the target text) of that alignment and vice versa. In case a term-translation cannot be detected, the ITDB tries to prove the presence of a variant.

5 Abduction of Term Variants

As outlined in section 3, abduction of term variants in the ITDB presupposes a bilingual terminology. In an evaluation scenario which we shall describe in this section, a bilingual terminology was manually extracted from a text SNIPER2 (cf. section 6). The bilingual terminology contains 168 non-ambiguous term translations where each LHS and each RHS occurs exactly once in the terminology.

Synonyms of the term's content words were generated automatically from a bilingual dictionary by back-and-forth translating[4]. For instance, the terms (7), (8) and (9) in figure 2 were manually extracted from SNIPER2. The terms (7) and (8) contain as their head words the translation *ring* ↔ bague. Back-and-forth translation of French bague yields 29 synonyms while through back-and-forth translation of English *ring* 45 synonyms were generated. In this way, variants (7_{LHS_0}) are recognized as variants of the English term in (7) and variants (7_{RHS_0}) are recognized as variants of the French term in (7). In all, 549 and 650 synonyms were generated from the 168 English and French terms.

In addition to this, a number of variation pattern were used to abduce further variants. Currently, we have the following two simple varia-

[4]We used a general-purpose English-French dictionary with 77016 entries. Lists of English synonyms were obtained by looking up their French translations and then back-translating each of the French translations into English using the same dictionary. In future we consider to use WordNet to obtain synonyms of the term's content words.

tion pattern for French omission (1) and insertion (2) variation :

$$(1) \quad N_1 p \ldots \rightarrow N_1$$
$$(2) \quad N_1 Adj_2 \rightarrow N_1 xy Adj_2$$

These variation pattern produced 131 additional variants for the French terms. For instance, the omission variant (7_{RHS_1}) was abduced using variation pattern (1) while insertion variant (9_{RHS_2}) was abduced using variation pattern (2). The tag xy matches any sequence of two words such that, for instance, mouvement vers l'arrière is abduced as a variant of (9). For the English side, only synonyms, but no variation pattern were generated.

While the original terminology contains only $1 - to - 1$ term translations, abduction generates $m - to - n$ translation relations. Thus due to variation pattern (1), French bague is recognized as an omission variant either of term (7) or of term (8). Accordingly, the translations may be English *focusing ring* or *eyepiece locking ring*. Unless another translation is known, the same translation is also abduced for the synonyms: anneau;aggraver;bouche;boucle;.... Abduction thus enables m different French expressions to be translated into n different English terms. However, adding further terms to the terminology will narrow the number of generated translations, as a terminology entry will be preferred over an abduced variant if they describe the same surface string.

6 Coverage and Precision of ITDB

The ITDB was tested on two texts, SNIPER2 and SNIPER3. The texts are an excerpt of an army manual on sniper training and deployment that was used in an other study (Macklovitch, 1995). This corpus is highly specific to the military domain and would certainly prove difficult to any translation engine not specifically tuned to such material.

SNIPER2 and SNIPER3 have 391 and 916 French-English aligned sentences, respectively with an average length of 19 and 22 words in the English LHS and the French RHS. Note that the terminology was also extracted from SNIPER2.

Both language sides of the two texts were passed through the ITDB in two different ways: once only the authorized terms (T) and another time the authorized terms and their abduced variants (T+A) were were marked in both language sides of the aligned texts and retrieved from the output of the evaluation architecture (cf. figure 1). To measure the gain in coverage and precision, we have counted the noise produced in the English and French sides as well as the valid recovered translations equivalences. The table 1 summarizes the results. The row E indicates the noise on the English side of the alignments, i.e the number of matched English expressions which have no correspondences in the French side of the alignment. The row F indicates the noise on the French side. The row $E \leftrightarrow F$ gives the number of valid translations in the alignment.

	SNIPER2		SNIPER3	
	T	T+A	T	T+A
E	131	78	396	343
F	74	220	166	666
$E \leftrightarrow F$	528	638	783	948
PE	0.80	0.90	0.66	0.73
PF	0.87	0.74	0.83	0.59

Table 1: Coverage and Precision of the ITDB

.

In SNIPER2, 659 English terms (i.e. $E \leftrightarrow F + E$) and 602 French terms (i.e. $E \leftrightarrow F + F$) were found using the terminology only, while 716 English and 858 French expressions were matched with abduced variants. Of these matched terms and expressions 528 and 638 were valid translations. This equals a gain of 120% in coverage when using abduced variants.

A similar situation appears for SNIPER3, where 948 valid translations were found using abduced variants compared to 783 translation equivalences for the terminology only. This amounts to an increase of 121% coverage compared to the terminology.

SNIPER	T-T	1-S	S-S	1-T	S-T	2-T
2	528	17	6	80	6	1
3	782	28	10	102	26	0

Table 2: Types and Number of Abduced Translation Equivalences

Analysing the abduced translation equivalences for SNIPER2 and SNIPER3 (cf. table 2), we

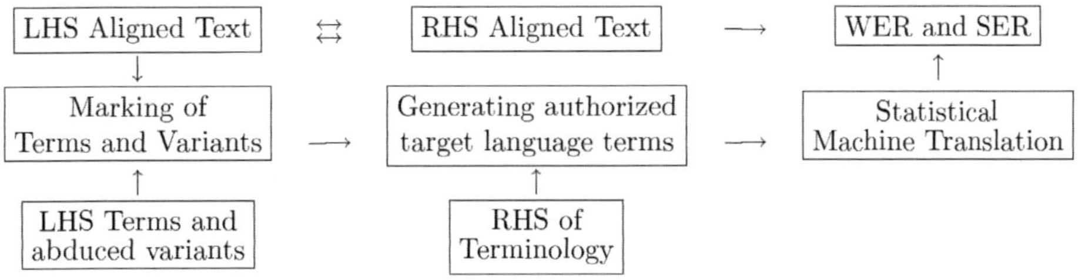

Figure 3: Runtime architecture of the ITDB.

find the 528 and 783[5] French-English term—term translations (T-T) amongst the the 638 and 948 valid translations. In addition there are 17 and 28 omission-variant—synonym (1-S) translations and 6 and 10 synonym—synonym (S-S) translations and 87 and 127 variant—term (1-T, S-T and 2-T) translations.

By far most of the abduced translation equivalences are due to variation pattern (1)—i.e. the French/English translations 1-S and 1-T—which generates 97 and 130 additional translation equivalences for SNIPER2 and SNIPER3.

However, variation pattern (1) also generates most of the noise in the French alignments. The rows PE and PF in table 1 indicate precision for the English side of alignments calculated as $PE = \frac{E\leftrightarrow F}{E\leftrightarrow F+E}$ and for the French side of alignments calculated as $PF = \frac{E\leftrightarrow F}{E\leftrightarrow F+E}$.

While the precision of the matched English terms increases when matching abduced variants, the precision of the French terms decreases.

	SNIPER2		SNIPER3			
	T	1	T	1	S	2
E	78	0	316	0	27	0
F	68	152	157	492	12	5

Table 3: Origin of Noise in Alignments

Examining the origin of noise in alignments (cf. table 3), more than 2/3 of the matched French sequences which have no correspondence on the English side of the alignment are due to variation pattern 1. As discussed previously (cf. figure 2), each occurrence of the word bouche in the French side of an alignment produces noise if no variant of *focusing ring* or *eyepiece locking ring* was found in the English side of that alignment. This clearly indicates that the variation pattern (1) is too simple — specially if combined with a noisy list of synonyms — which calls for further refinement.

In order to reduce this noise and to extend the coverage of the ITDB, future work will be in line with the methodology of iterative refinement as outlined by Meyer (Meyer, 2001).

7 Integrating ITDB and STM

In a second experiment we have linked the ITDB with an SMT system. The way the ITDB interacts with the SMT engine is depicted in the block diagram of Figure 3. The ITDB identifies and marks terms and their possible variants in the source text (LHS Aligned Text) and regenerates their authorized target language form. The marked and with target language segments enriched text is then passed through the SMT system as described in (Langlais, 2002). While the position of the target term in the French target sentence is determined by the SMT system, its form is generated by the ITDB[6]. in the French alignments . The output of the SMT is then compared with an oracle translation i.e. the RHS Aligned Text.

As in the previous experiment, the architecture was tested on SNIPER2 and SNIPER3, this time in three different settings: without any terminological lexicon, with the terminology (T) and with both the terminology and its abduced variants (T+A). The results of the translation sessions are resumed in Table 4. For practical reasons, we only translated the sentences that contained at most 30 words.

[5]The table 2 shows the number 782: I could not figure out where the missing translation equivalent disappeared ...

[6]Texts were translated from English to French so that the noisy French terms, as reported in the previous section, would not be generated.

	WITHOUT		T		T+A	
corpus	SER	WER	SER	WER	SER	WER
SNIPER2	86.8	82.9	82.6	77.1	82.5	76.6
SNIPER3	91.8	82	91.8	79.4	91.8	79.4

Table 4: SMT Results with the ITDB as a Preprocessor

The performance of our engine was evaluated in terms of `word error rate` (WER) and `sentence error rate` (SER) according to a single oracle translation. The former rate is computed by a classical Levenstein distance; the latter one is given by the ratio of translation that were strictly identical to the oracle translation.

First, the WER measured without terminology is fairly high (more than 82% for both corpora), but in the same range as the ones observed by (Langlais, 2002) in cases where the decoder is faced to texts very different from the ones used at training time. The introduction of the terminology into the engine improves significantly the WER (77% on SNIPER2 and 79.4% on SNIPER3).

Finally, the further introduction of the terminological variants does have a slight positive impact on SNIPER2, but none on SNIPER-3. We have currently no convincing explanation for these findings. We must stress that WER computed over a single oracle translation is probably severe: it may happen that an authorized term translation proposed by the ITDB was not the one present in the oracle translation. This degrades WER even though a correct (i.e. more consistent) translation was produced than was contained in the oracle translation.

8 Conclusion

The paper presents an Intelligent Terminological Database (ITDB), a tool to detect terms and their variants in texts and to retrieve their authorized translations from a bilingual terminology. The paper outlines the architecture of the ITDB and reports on two experiments. The first experiment quantifies the coverage and precision for detecting terminological variants and their translations in aligned texts. In the second experiment, the ITDB is used to translate terms and their variants as a pre-processor for a statistical machine translation system. While the first experiment shows encouraging results, the success of the ITDB as a pre-processor for a statistical machine translation seems more doubtful. A thorough revision and modification of the interaction of both systems is probably in order to fully complement the strength of the two systems. Further experimentation and refinement is also required to reduce the noise produced by the ITDB and to augment its coverage.

References

Didier Bourigault, Christian Jacquemin, and Mairie-Claude L'Homme. 2001. *Recent Advances in Computational Terminology.* John Benjamins Publishing Company, Amsterdam/Philadelphia.

Peter F. Brown, Stephen A. Della Pietra, Vincent J. Della Pietra, Meredith J. Goldsmith, Jan Hajic, Robert L. Mercer, and Surya Mohanty. 1993. But dictionaries are data too. In *Human Language Technology (HLT)*, pages 202–205, Princeton, NJ, march.

Michael Carl, Johann Haller, Christoph Horschmann, Dieter Maas, and Jörg Schütz. 2002. The TETRIS Terminology Tool. *TAL*, Structuration de terminologie(1).

Thierry Hamon and Adeline Nazarenko. 2001. Detection of synonymy links between terms: Experiment and results. In *in (Bourigault et al., 2001)*, pages 185–208.

Christian Jacquemin. 1996. A symbolic and surgical acquisition of terms through variation. In *Connectionist, Statistical and Symbolic Approaches to Learning for Natural Language Processing*, pages 425–438.

Philipe Langlais. 2002. Ressources terminologiques et traduction probabiliste: premiers pas positifs vers un système adaptatif. In *TALN.*

Elliott Macklovitch. 1995. Can terminological consistency be validated automatically ? Technical report, CITI/RALI, Montréal, Canada.

Ingrid Meyer. 2001. Extracting knowledge-rich contexts for terminography. In *in (Bourigault et al., 2001)*, pages 279–302.

Raymond J. Mooney. 2000. Integrating abduction and induction in machine learning. In P. Flach and A. Kakas, editors, *Abduction and Induction*, pages 181–191, Kluwer Academic Publishers.

F.J. Och and H. Ney. 2000. A comparison of alignement models for statistical machine translation. In *COLING00*, pages 1086–1090.

Oliver Streiter. 2001. Treebank Development with Deductive and Abductive Explanation-based Learning: Exploratory Experiments. unpublished draft.

Lexically-Based Terminology Structuring: Some Inherent Limits

Natalia Grabar and **Pierre Zweigenbaum**
STIM/DSI, Assistance Publique – Hôpitaux de Paris
& Département de Biomathématiques, Université Paris 6
{ngr,pz}@biomath.jussieu.fr
http://www.biomath.jussieu.fr/~{ngr,pz}

Abstract

Terminology structuring has been the subject of much work in the context of terms extracted from corpora: given a set of terms, obtained from an existing resource or extracted from a corpus, identifying hierarchical (or other types of) relations between these terms. The present paper focusses on terminology structuring by lexical methods, which match terms on the basis on their content words, taking morphological variants into account. Experiments are done on a 'flat' list of terms obtained from an originally hierarchically-structured terminology: the French version of the US National Library of Medicine MeSH thesaurus. We compare the lexically-induced relations with the original MeSH relations: after a quantitative evaluation of their congruence through recall and precision metrics, we perform a qualitative, human analysis of the 'new' relations not present in the MeSH. This analysis shows, on the one hand, the limits of the lexical structuring method. On the other hand, it also reveals some specific structuring choices and naming conventions made by the MeSH designers, and emphasizes ontological commitments that cannot be left to automatic structuring.

1 Background

Terminology structuring, *i.e.*, organizing a set of terms through semantic relations, is one of the difficult issues that have to be addressed when building terminological resources. These relations include subsumption or hyperonymy (the *is-a* relation), meronymy (*part-of* and its variants), as well as other, diverse relations, sometimes called 'transversal' (*e.g.*, *cause*, or the general *see also*).

Various methods have been proposed to discover relations between terms (see Jacquemin and Bourigault (2002) for a review). We divide them into *internal* and *external* methods, in the same way as McDonald (1993) for proper names. Internal methods look at the constituency of terms, and compare terms based on the words they contain. Term matching can rely directly on raw word forms (Bodenreider et al., 2001), on morphological variants (Jacquemin and Tzoukermann, 1999), on syntactic structure (Bourigault, 1994; Jacquemin and Tzoukermann, 1999) or on semantic variants (synonyms, hyperonyms, etc.) (Hamon et al., 1998). External methods take advantage of the context in which terms occur: they examine the behavior of terms in corpora. Distributional methods group terms that occur in similar contexts (Grefenstette, 1994). The detection of appropriate syntactic patterns of cooccurrence is another method to uncover relations between terms in corpora (Hearst, 1992; Séguéla and Aussenac, 1999).

In previous work we applied lexical methods to identify relations between terms on the basis on their content words, taking morphological variants into account. Our goal was then to assess the feasibility of such structuring by studying it on an existing, hierarchically structured terminology. Ignoring this existing structure and starting from the set of its terms, we attempt to discover hierarchical term-to-term links and compare them with the preexisting relations.

Our goal in the present paper is to analyze 'new' relations. 'New' means that these induced relations are not present in the original hierarchical structure of the MeSH thesaurus; they might nevertheless reflect useful links. Performing this analysis allows us to propose a more precise evaluation of the methods and their results and to point out some inherent limits.

After the exposition of the data we used in our experiments (section 2), we present methods (section 3) for generating hierarchical links between terms through the study of lexical inclusion and for evaluating their quality with appropriate recall and precision metrics. We then present the analysis of some 'new' induced relations and attempt to propose a typology of term dependency in these relations (section 4). We finally discuss the limits of lexical methods for the structuring task (section 5).

2 The MeSH biomedical thesaurus, and associated morphological knowledge

We first present the existing hierarchically structured thesaurus, a 'stop word' list and morphological knowledge involved in the present work.

2.1 The MeSH biomedical thesaurus

The Medical Subject Headings (MeSH, NLM (2001a)) is one of the main international medical terminologies (see, *e.g.*, Cimino (1996) for a presentation of medical terminologies). It is a thesaurus specifically designed for information retrieval in the biomedical domain. The MeSH is used to index the international biomedical literature in the Medline bibliographic database. The French version of the MeSH (INSERM, 2000) contains a translation of these terms (19,638 terms) plus synonyms. It happens to be written in unaccented, uppercase letters. Both the American and French MeSH can be found in the UMLS Metathesaurus (NLM, 2001b), which can be obtained through a convention with the National Library of Medicine.

The concept names (*main headings*) which the MeSH contains have been designed to reflect their broad meanings and to facilitate their use by human indexers and librarians. In that, they follow a tradition in information sciences, and are not necessarily the expressions used in naturally occurring biomedical documents. The MeSH can be considered as a fine-grained thesaurus: concepts are chosen to insure a good coverage of the biomedical domain (Zweigenbaum, 1999).

As many other medical terminologies, the MeSH has a hierarchical structure: 'narrower' concepts (children) are related to 'broader' concepts (parents). This both covers the usual *is-a* relation and partitive relations (*part-of*, *conceptual-part-of* and *process-of*). The MeSH also includes *see-also* relations, which we do not take into account in the present experiments. This structure has also been designed in the aim to be intellectually accessible to users: an indexer must be able to assign a given concept to an article and a clinician must be able to find a given concept in the tree hierarchy (Nelson et al., 2001). To conclude, the MeSH team aims to organize it in a clear and intuitive manner, both for concept naming and concept placement.

The version of the French MeSH we used in these experiments contains 19,638 terms, 26,094 direct child-to-parent links and (under transitive closure) 95,815 direct or indirect child-to-ancestor links.

2.2 Stop word list

The aim of using a 'stop word' list is to remove from term comparison very frequent words which are considered not to be content-bearing, hence 'non-significant' for terminology structuring. We used in this experiment a short stop word list (15 word forms). It contains the few frequent grammatical words, such as articles and prepositions, that occur in MeSH terms.

2.3 Morphological knowledge

The morphological knowledge involved consists of *lemma/derived-word* or *lemma/inflected form* pairs where the first is the 'normalized' form and the second a 'variant' form.

Inflection produces the various forms of a given word such as plural, feminine or the multiple forms of a verb according to person, tense, etc.: *intervention – interventions*, *acid – acids*. We perform the reverse process (lemmatization), reducing an inflected form to its lemma (canonical form). We worked with two alternate lexicons. The first one is based on a general French lexicon (ABU, abu.cnam.fr/DICO) which we have augmented with pairs obtained from medical corpora processed through a tagger/lemmatizer (in cardiology, hematology, intensive care, and drug monographs): it totals 219,759 pairs (where the inflected form is different from the lemma). The second lexicon, more specialized and tuned to the vocabulary in medical terminologies, is the result of applying rules acquired in previous work from two other medical terminologies (ICD-10 and SNOMED) to the vocabulary in the MeSH, ICD-10 and SNOMED (total: 2,889 pairs).

Derivation produces, *e.g.*, the adjectival form of a noun (noun *aorta* ↔ adjective *aortic*), the nominal form of a verb (verb *intervene* ↔ noun *intervention*), or the adverbial form of an adjective (adjective *human* ↔ adverb *humanely*). We perform linguistically-motivated stemming to reduce a derived word to its base word. For derivation, we also used resources acquired in previous work which, once combined with inflection pairs, results in 4,517 pairs.

Compounding, which combines several radicals, often of Greek or Latin origin, to obtain complex words (*e.g.*, *aorta* + *coronary* yields *aortocoronary*), has not been used because we do not have a reliable procedure to segment a compound into its component morphemes.

3 Acquiring links through lexical inclusion of terms

The present work induces hierarchical relations between terms when the constituent words of one term lexically include those of the second term (section 3.1). When comparing these relations with those that preexist in the MeSH, precision can reach 29.3% and recall 13.7% (section 3.2). We focus here on the analysis of the relations that are not found in the MeSH (section 3.3), which we develop in the next section (section 4).

3.1 Lexical inclusion

The method we use here for inducing hierarchical relations between terms is basically a test of *lexical inclusion*: we check whether a term P (*parent*) is 'included' in another term C (*child*), *i.e.*, whether all words in P occur in C. We assume that this type of inclusion is a clue of a hierarchical relation between terms, as in *acides gras / acides gras indispensables* (*fatty acids / fatty acids, essential*).

To detect this type of relation, we test whether all the content words of P occur in C. We do this on segmented terms with a gradually increasing normalization on word forms. Basic normalizations are performed first: conversion to lower case, removal of punctuation, of numbers and of 'stop words'. Subsequent normalizations rely on morphological ressources: lemmatization (with the two alternate inflectional lexicons) and stemming with a derivational lexicon. Terms are indexed by their words to speed up the computation of term inclusion over all term pairs of the whole MeSH thesaurus.

3.2 Application to MeSH and quantification

This structuring method has been applied to the flat list of 19,638 terms of the MeSH thesaurus. As expected, the number of links induced between terms increases when applying inflectional normalization and again with derivational normalization.

We evaluated the quality of the links obtained with this approach by comparing them automatically with the original structure of the MeSH and computing recall and precision metrics. We summarize here the main results; a detailed evaluation can be found in (Grabar and Zweigenbaum, 2002).

Depending on the normalization, up to 29.3% of the links found are correct (precision), and up to 13.7% of the direct MeSH links are found by lexical inclusion (recall). We also examined whether each term was correctly placed under one of its ancestors: this was true for up to 26% of the terms (recall); and the placement advices were correct in up to 58% of the cases (precision). The recall of links increases when applying more complete morphological knowledge (inflection then derivation). The evolution of precision is opposite: injection of more extensive morphological knowledge (derivation *vs* inflection) leads to taking more 'chances' for generating links between terms: the precision with no normalization (*raw* results) is 29.3% *vs* 22.5% when using all normalizations (*lem-stem-med*). Depending on the type of normalization, the best precision obtained for links is 43%.

3.3 Human analysis of 'new' relations

The evaluations presented in the previous section quantify the match between the induced relations and existing MeSH relations. However, they give no explanation for the fact that 70% of the induced relations are not considered relevant by the MeSH. This is what we study in the remainder of this paper: why these terms are not hierarchically related in the MeSH, and what kinds of relations exist between them.

According to the position of the words of the 'parent' term in the 'child' term, we divide the extra-MeSH relations into three sets: (1) the parent concept is at the *head* position in the child concept: *absorption/absorption intestinale*; (2) the parent concept is at the tail (*expansion*) position in the child concept: *abdomen/tumeur abdomen*; (3) *other* types of positions. Each set of relations is sampled by randomly selecting a 20% subset, both without normalization (*raw*) and with inflectional and derivational normalizations (*med-lem-stem*). Table 1 presents the number of analyzed relations (total = 194).

Normalizations	Head	Expan.	Other
raw	22	31	14
lem-stem-med	37	57	33

Table 1: Relations to analyze: sample sizes.

4 An analysis of new, lexically-induced relations

We first examine the issues encountered when trying to identify the head of each term (section 4.1), then review in turn each analyzed subset: head (section 4.2), expansion (section 4.3) and other relations (section 4.4).

4.1 Finding the head

In French, the semantic head of a noun phrase is usually located at the beginning of this phrase (this contrasts with English, where the semantic head is generally at the end of NPs). Moreover, as is often the case with terms, MeSH terms do not include determiners, so that the semantic head is usually the first word here. We therefore rely on a heuristic for determining 'head' and 'expansion' subsets: the head is the first word of the term, and the expansion is the last word. This is correct most of the time, but in some cases, the semantic head is positioned at the end of the term, generally separated with a comma, a tradition sometimes followed in thesauri:

filoviridae/filoviridae, infections,
leishmania/leishmania tropica, infection,
quinones/quinone reductases,
neurone/neurone moteur, maladie,
syndrome/bouche main pied, syndrome.

These cases must be hand-corrected and distributed into the following classes.

We also encountered another kind of error, due to overzealous derivational knowledge:

contracture/contraction musculaire,
biologie/testament biologique,

where *contracture* (a muscle disease) and *contraction* (normal muscle function) have both been stemmed to the same base word; the expansion adjective *biologique* is derived from the noun *biologie*, but its sense is generally more specific than *biologie*.

4.2 'Head' subset

Let us first discard a case where it seems that we encountered a translation error. An examination of the structure of the English MeSH and a search on Web pages show that in the French MeSH, *acide linoleique alpha* should read *acide linolenique alpha*, which is a kind of *acide linolenique* (and not a kind of *acide linoleique*). The induced relation:

acide linoleique/acide linoleique alpha

is therefore incorrect; with the correct spelling, the lexical inclusion:

acide linolenique/acide linolenique alpha

would reveal a correct hierarchical relation.

4.2.1 The head is not the 'genus' of the term

We encountered cases where the whole term did not have an *is-a* relation with the head as defined above. This happens in two types of situations.

The first situation is due to syntactic reasons. In the following induced relation,

acides amines / acides amines, peptides et proteines,

the larger term is an enumeration, with the sense of a logical OR. It is therefore the genus term, of which each of its components (*e.g.*, *acides amines*) is a sub-type.

The second situation is due to semantic reasons. Lexical induction of hierarchical relations assumes inheritance of the defining features of the genus term (*e.g.*, a *fatty acid, essential* is a kind of *fatty acid*). However, it is well known that this is not always true: a *plaster cat* is not a *cat* (*i.e.*, a mammal, etc.). This is sometimes modeled as a type coercion phenomenon. We found quite a few 'plaster cats' in our terms:

personnalite/personnalite compulsive,
voix/voix oesophagienne.

For instance, *personnalite* here describes 'behavior-response patterns that characterize the individual', whereas *personnalite compulsive* (*compulsive personality disorder*) describes a mental disorder. Disorders (or diseases) are different objects than behaviors in the MeSH.

4.2.2 The head is ambiguous

This depends on the choice of term names in the terminology (here, the MeSH). Terms like *absorption*, *investissement*, etc., have specific senses that make them polysemous. To determine a precise sense, these terms have to be specialized by their contexts:

investissement/investissement (psychanalyse),
absorption/absorption cutanee,
goitre/goitre ovarien

Here, *investissement* alone (*investment*) has the financial sense, whereas in *investissement (psychanalyse)*, it has its more generic sense. In a similar way, *absorption* has a specific meaning in chemistry, and *goitre* alone is a disorder of the thyroid gland. These cases are often non-ambiguous in the original English version of the same terms: for instance, *investissement (psychanalyse)* (fr) is a translation of *cathexis* (en).

A related case occurs when the name of a parent term is underspecified:

acides/acides pentanoiques,
acne/acne rosacee.

In these examples, *acides* means *inorganic acids*[1] and *acne* means *acne vulgaris*, but the convention adopted is to use these single words to name the corresponding concepts.

4.2.3 Ontological commitment

Finally, some induced links, although absent from the MeSH, are potentially correct *is-a* links, but the designers of the MeSH have made a different modeling choice:

amyotrophies/amyotrophies spinales enfance,
hyperplasie/hyperplasie epitheliale focale,
centre public sante/centre public sante mentale,
rectocolite/rectocolite hemorragique,
penicillines/penicilline g.

A general representational choice in the MeSH, as in some other medical terminologies (*e.g.*, SNOMED), is to differentiate on the one hand *signs or symptoms* and on the other hand *diseases* (a more fully characterized pathological state). This is the case for *amyotrophies* and *hyperplasie* (*signs or symptoms*) *vs amyotrophies spinales enfance* and *hyperplasie epitheliale focale* (*disease* of the nervous system, of the mouth).

For some reason, a *centre public sante mentale* (public mental health center) is considered not to share all the attributes of a general *centre public sante* (public health center), which prevents them from being in a parent-child relationship: they are only siblings in the MeSH thesaurus.

Penicillines, in the MeSH, have been chosen to refer to a therapeutic class of drugs (under *antibiotics*, under *chemical actions*), whereas *penicilline g* is considered as a chemical substance.

The structuring involved in these instances reflects the ontological commitments of the terminology designers, and cannot be recovered by lexical inclusion.[2]

4.3 'Expansion' subset

When a 'parent' term is in 'expansion' position (end position) in a 'child' term, we assume that the semantic head of the child term is modified; the induced relation is indeed expected not to be *is-a*. Some of the main cases found are close to those for the 'head' subset. Among others, we find again enumerations (see subsection 4.2.1):

immunodepresseurs / antineoplasiques et immunodepresseurs

and syntactic ambiguity (subsection 4.2.2):

oncogene/antigene viral oncogene,

where the word *oncogene* is a noun in the first term and an adjective in the second one.

Many of the relations found in the 'expansion' subset are partitive:

abdomen/muscle droit abdomen,
amerique centrale/indien amerique centrale,
argent/nitrate argent.

(human body parts, a continent and its peoples, and chemical substances).

In some instances, a general type of link between terms can be detected:

caused-by: *myxome/virus myxome,*

but in most other cases, we have what looks like a specific thematic relation between a predicate and its argument:

comportement alimentaire/troubles comportement alimentaire,
bovin/pneumonie interstitielle atypique bovin,
hopital/capacite lits hopital,
services sante/fermeture service sante,
macrophage/activation macrophage.

Note that some of these expansion relations involve adjectival derivations of nouns:

cubitus/nerf cubital,
genes/epreuve complementation genetique.

[1]Note, though, that if *inorganic acids* was named this way, it would be impossible to link it by lexical induction to other, more specific types of inorganic acids.

[2]They might be amenable to distributional methods if their contexts of occurrence are different enough.

4.4 'Other' subset

In this last subset, the 'parent' term can be at any position in the 'child' term other than head or expansion. It can also be non-contiguous, accepting modifiers or some other intervening elements. All these cases are actually similar to those of the 'expansion' subset except those of the form:

bacterie aerobie/bacterie gram-negatif aerobie

where *bacterie* remains the head of the term.

The following examples reproduce the general cases of the 'expansion' subset with additional modifiers:

arteres/anevrysme artere iliaque,
hepatite b/virus hepatite b canard,
encephalite/virus encephalite equine ouest,
sommeil/troubles sommeil extrinseques,
irrigation/liquide irrigation endocanalaire,
maladie/assurance maladie personne agee.

In some of them, adjectival derivation is involved:

cellules/molecule-1 adhesion cellulaire vasculaire,
chimie/produits chimiques inorganiques,
dent/implantation dentaire sous-periostee.

Some relations are characteristic of the language of chemical compounds:

cytochrome c/ubiquinol-cytochrome c reductase,
diphosphate/uridine diphosphate acide glucuronique,
lysine/histone-lysine n-methyltransferase.

The 'other' subset also hosted the following morphosyntactic ambiguity:

cilie/cellule ciliee externe

where the words *cilie* (noun, an invertebrate organism) and *ciliee* (inflected form of adjective *cilie*, which characterizes a type of cell) are conflated by lemmatization. This error is mainly due to the fact that the MeSH is written with unaccented uppercase letters: the adjective is actually spelled *cilié*, which would be unambiguous here.

5 Synthesis

We presented in this paper a human analysis of automatically, lexically-induced term relations that were not found in the terminology from which the terms were obtained (the MeSH thesaurus). This lexical method considers that a term P is probably a parent of a term C iff all the words of P occur in C. This inclusion test is helped by morphological normalization.

Morphological normalization was found to be useful not only in identifying the already existing relations (section 3.2), but also for the 'new' relations. This confirms previous work by Jacquemin and Tzoukermann (1999).

The occurrences of syntactic ambiguity suggest that morphosyntactic tagging could be useful. The methods specifically designed for detection of syntactic and morphosyntactic term variants (Bourigault, 1994; Jacquemin and Tzoukermann, 1999) might then be more efficient and less error-prone. We must be warned however that this may not be an easy task, since most of the MeSH terms are not syntactically well-formed (few determiners and prepositions, inverted heads) and contain rare, technical words that are likely to be absent from most electronic lexicons.

Spurious relations may come from several sources. A few cases are due to abusive morphological normalization; errors in term names (translation errors) were also uncovered. We made a distinction between 'head' and 'expansion' positions of the 'parent' term in its 'child'. One would expect that relations where the parent is in head position would be correct; however, this is not always true.

The putative head of a term is sometimes not correctly identified because of specific thesaural constructs (the 'comma' form) and chemical constructs (*quinone reductases* are a kind of *reductases*) which display head inversion, and because of enumerations. An additional situation is that of a term whose actual syntactic head does not entertain an *is-a* relation with it (the 'plaster cat'). Furthermore, the head word may not have a stable meaning: it may be syntactically ambiguous (*cilie*), polysemous (*investissement*) or underspecified (*acne*).

The remaining 'head' cases reveal specific modeling options, or 'ontological commitments', of the terminology designers: the relations induced might be considered semantically valid, but were discarded in the MeSH because of overall structuring choices. These choices cannot be predicted with the lexical methods used here, and seem to be the most resistant to attempts at automatic derivation. They also show that what is correct is not necessarily useful for a given terminology.

The 'expansion' cases may be useful to propose other relations than *is-a*: we displayed partitive relations, but left to further work a classification of the remaining ones. The UMLS semantic network relations (NLM, 2001b) might be a relevant direction to look into to represent such links.

References

Olivier Bodenreider, Anita Burgun, and Thomas C. Rindflesch. 2001. Lexically-suggested hyponymic relations among medical terms and their representation in the UMLS. In URI INIST CNRS, editor, *TIA'2001 Terminologie et Intelligence artificielle*, pages 11–21, Nancy.

Didier Bourigault. 1994. Extraction et structuration automatiques de terminologie pour l'aide à l'acquisition de connaissances à partir de textes. In *Proceedings of the 9 th Conference RFIA-AFCET*, pages 1123–1132, Paris, France, January. AFCET.

James J Cimino. 1996. Coding systems in health care. In Jan H. van Bemmel and Alexa T. McCray, editors, *Yearbook of Medical Informatics '95 — The Computer-based Patient Record*, pages 71–85. Schattauer, Stuttgart.

Natalia Grabar and Pierre Zweigenbaum. 2002. Lexically-based terminology structuring: a feasibility study. In *LREC Workshop on Using Semantics for Information Retrieval and Filtering*, pages 73–77, Las Palmas, Canaries, May. ELRA.

Gregory Grefenstette. 1994. *Explorations in Automatic Thesaurus Discovery*. Natural Language Processing and Machine Translation. Kluwer Academic Publishers, London.

Thierry Hamon, Adeline Nazarenko, and Cécile Gros. 1998. A step towards the detection of semantic variants of terms in technical documents. In Christian Boitet, editor, *Proceedings of the 17 th COLING*, pages 498–504, Montréal, Canada, 10–14 August.

Marti A. Hearst. 1992. Automatic acquisition of hyponyms from large text corpora. In Antonio Zampolli, editor, *Proceedings of the 14 th COLING*, pages 539–545, Nantes, France, 23–28 July.

INSERM, 2000. *Thésaurus Biomédical Français/Anglais*. Institut National de la Santé et de la Recherche Médicale, Paris.

Christian Jacquemin and Didier Bourigault. 2002. Term extraction and automatic indexing. In Ruslan Mitkov, editor, *Handbook of Computational Linguistics*. Oxford University Press, Oxford. *To appear*.

Christian Jacquemin and Évelyne Tzoukermann. 1999. NLP for term variant extraction: A synergy of morphology, lexicon, and syntax. In Tomek Strzalkowski, editor, *Natural language information retrieval*, volume 7 of *Text, speech and language technology*, chapter 2, pages 25–74. Kluwer Academic Publishers, Dordrecht & Boston.

David D. McDonald. 1993. Internal and external evidence in the identification and semantic categorization of proper names. In Branimir Boguraev and James Pustejovsky, editors, *Corpus Processing for Lexical Acquisition*, pages 61–76. MIT Press, Cambridge, MA.

Stuart J Nelson, Douglas Johnston, and Betsy L Humphreys. 2001. Relationships in medical subject headings. In Carol A Bean and Rebecca Green, editors, *Relationships in the organization of knowledge*, New York. Kluwer Academic Publishers.

National Library of Medicine, Bethesda, Maryland, 2001a. *Medical Subject Headings*. www.nlm.nih.gov/mesh/meshhome.html.

National Library of Medicine, Bethesda, Maryland, 2001b. *UMLS Knowledge Sources Manual*. www.nlm.nih.gov/research/umls/.

Patrick Séguéla and Nathalie Aussenac. 1999. Extraction de relations sémantiques entre termes et enrichissement de modèles du domaine. In Régine Teulier, editor, *Actes de IC'99*, June.

Pierre Zweigenbaum. 1999. Encoder l'information médicale : des terminologies aux systèmes de représentation des connaissances. *Innovation Stratégique en Information de Santé*, (2–3):27–47.

Alignment and Extraction of Bilingual Legal Terminology from Context Profiles

Oi Yee Kwong, Benjamin K. Tsou, Tom B.Y. Lai, Robert W.P. Luk[†],
Lawrence Y.L. Cheung and **Francis C.Y. Chik**

Language Information Sciences Research Centre
City University of Hong Kong
Tat Chee Avenue, Kowloon, Hong Kong
{rlolivia,rlbtsou,cttomlai,rlylc,rlfchik}@cityu.edu.hk

[†]Department of Computing
Hong Kong Polytechnic University
Hung Hom, Kowloon, Hong Kong
csrluk@comp.polyu.edu.hk

Abstract

In this study, we propose a knowledge-independent method for aligning terms and thus extracting translations from a small, domain-specific corpus consisting of parallel English and Chinese court judgments from Hong Kong. With a sentence-aligned corpus, translation equivalences are suggested by analysing the frequency profiles of parallel concordances. The method overcomes the limitations of conventional statistical methods which require large corpora to be effective, and lexical approaches which depend on existing bilingual dictionaries. Pilot testing on a parallel corpus of about 113K Chinese words and 120K English words gives an encouraging 85% precision and 45% recall. Future work includes fine-tuning the algorithm upon the analysis of the errors, and acquiring a translation lexicon for legal terminology by filtering out general terms.

1 Introduction

Machine translation, parallel text alignment, and translation lexicons are the vertices in their tightly bound triangular relation. The mutual relation between translation lexicons and parallel text alignment is especially close as they together provide foundational resources for the research of machine translation.

Conventional statistical methods for bilingual word alignment and extraction of translation lexicon require large corpora to be effective. Lexical approaches, on the other hand, depend on existing bilingual dictionaries which often only cover general terms. In any case, both methods will probably fall short with a small and domain-specific corpus, as the one in our study.

The parallel corpus in this study consists of bilingual Hong Kong court judgments, in English and Chinese. It is a small and domain-specific corpus. Thus on the one hand, we can imagine that existing bilingual dictionaries would be of little help in the alignment process, as general lexicons do not often cover legal terminologies and their translations. On the other hand, the effectiveness of statistical or probabilistic approaches might not be realised, given the limited corpus size. Hence, neither approach fits the data ideally. Moreover, English and Chinese are from different language families. Also, legal terms are not limited to single words.

Hence, we propose a method for aligning terms in this small corpus of legal texts and extracting a translation lexicon therefrom, based on the consistency observed in legal texts. The method only requires a sentence-aligned corpus and suggests translation equivalences from the frequency profiles of parallel concordances. Pilot testing shows that the method is effective for fulfilling the two purposes, i.e. term alignment and lexicon extraction, simultaneously.

In the following, we will first review related studies in Section 2. Then we will describe the properties of our corpus in Section 3 and our method in Section 4. A pilot experiment with the proposed approach will be reported in Section 5 with results discussed in Section 6, followed by a conclusion in Section 7.

2 Related Work

Conventional bilingual sentence alignment is often based statistically on sentence length (e.g. Gale and Church, 1991), or lexically on cognates (e.g. Simard *et al.*, 1992) and correspondence of word position (e.g. Kay and Roescheisen, 1993; Piperidis *et al.*, 1997). Such criteria, however, are mostly applicable to Indo-European language pairs. Although Wu (1994) found the length criterion applied surprisingly well between English and Chinese, he supplemented the statistical, length-based method with lexical criteria. Fixed words or phrases with consistent translations, like month names, were identified first, and he observed an improvement of the results.

The derivation of bilingual dictionaries often follows text alignment (possibly at the word level) based on some frequency criterion. Nevertheless, in practice sentence alignment is not always distinctly separated from word alignment, and neither is word alignment and the derivation of translation lexicons thereby. In fact, apart from Gale and Church's length-based method, most other methods worked at the lexical level to some extent.

Word alignment can be done statistically by learning the translation association or token co-occurrences between the source language and the target language (e.g. Wu and Xia, 1995; Melamed, 1997). The acquisition of bilingual translation equivalences sometimes follows the acquisition of monolingual collocations (e.g. Wu and Xia, 1995; Smadja *et al.*, 1996). Wu and Xia (1995), for instance, made use of terms extracted by CXtract, a Chinese term extraction algorithm, to learn collocation translations for English words from the bilingual Hong Kong LegCo proceedings, reporting a precision of about 90%.

Others make use of existing bilingual dictionaries for word alignment, which is useful when the corpus is too small for statistical methods and contains many general words. For example, Ker and Chang (1997) worked with a small bilingual corpus (English-Chinese) and attempted to overcome the limitation of statistical methods by class-based rules, with reference to both an English and a Chinese machine readable dictionary.

When word alignment relies on existing lexical resources, however, the coverage tends toward the low end, probably due to the inherent limited coverage of existing resources. Huang and Choi (2000) used several linguistic resources, including bilingual and monolingual resources, for word alignment between Chinese and Korean texts. Even when they combined three algorithms together, there was still little improvement in coverage.

Using a third, pivot language as a bridge in word alignment may also improve the performance (e.g. Borin, 2000; Mann and Yarowsky, 2001). However, unlike Slavic languages or Indo-European languages, it seems difficult to imagine an effective bridge between English and Chinese.

Hybrid methods are also used (e.g. Piperidis *et al.*, 1997; Huang and Choi, 2000), and are believed to produce better alignment results.

Fung (1998), in contrast to the above which worked with parallel corpora, tried to extract bilingual lexicons from non-parallel corpora, which is more difficult. She discussed an algorithm called Convec, which compares the context vector of a given English word with the context vectors of all Chinese words for the most similar candidate. During the process, a bilingual dictionary is used to map the context words in the two languages. The method was about 30% accurate if the top-one candidate was considered, although the accuracy was more than doubled if the top-20 candidates were taken.

While most translation lexicon extraction methods do not particularly address domain-specificity, Resnik and Melamed (1997) suggested that a domain-specific translation lexicon could be obtained by filtering out general terms from the results. They, for instance, compared their extracted lexicon entries against a machine readable dictionary and discarded the terms in common.

In the next section, we will discuss our problem in this study and explain why existing methods are insufficient to solve it.

3 Characteristics of the Corpus

As mentioned earlier, we are working with a parallel corpus of bilingual Hong Kong court judgments. The following properties of the corpus render many existing word alignment and translation lexicon extraction methods limited in one way or another.

- **Small corpus size**

  The amount of bilingual Hong Kong court judgments is potentially growing, as long as there are legal proceedings. However, the part that is ready for use in this study only contains about 200K Chinese characters (about 113K word tokens upon segmentation) and about 120K English word tokens. This size is considered small, in view of the many large corpora in general domains available for natural language processing research, and may therefore not be ideal for many statistical methods.

- **Domain-specific corpus**

  The corpus consists of legal texts, and is thus very domain-specific. It would be a good resource from which to derive a legal translation lexicon. However, a lexical approach to alignment based on existing general bilingual dictionaries might be limited, because such dictionaries do not always cover legal terminologies and their translations. Even some general terms may be translated in special ways in legal texts.

- **Different language families**

  English and Chinese are from different language families and have little resemblance of each other. As a result, lexical criteria like cognates, or alignment via a bridging language will not be applicable.

- **Unpredictable word complexity**

  In many of the studies reviewed in Section 2, the alignment was confined to single words, at least for one of the languages in question (e.g. Wu and Xia, 1995; Melamed, 1997; Resnik and Melamed, 1997; Fung, 1998; Huang and Choi, 2000). For about 150 years, the legal system in Hong Kong operated through English only. So, many legal concepts may not be as precisely lexicalised in Chinese. The lengths and complexity of legal translations between English and Chinese are therefore not necessarily correlated. Aligning legal terms should therefore take care of the varying lengths and complexity of a source term and its translation equivalence.

3.1 Two Assumptions

On the other hand, we also have some advantages from the bilingual legal texts. Legal translations are well-known for their preciseness and consistency. Thus we make the following assumptions for the current study:

1. Bilingual legal texts form relatively clean parallel corpora, in the sense that the sentence alignments are expected to be neat, with few insertions and deletions.
2. Though not necessarily one sense per discourse, legal terms tend to be translated more consistently than common terms.

Based on these two assumptions, we propose a method, which depends minimally on prior knowledge, for aligning words and expressions in the corpus and thus extracting translation equivalences, as described in the next section.

4 Bilingual Term Alignment and Extraction

4.1 Task Definition

As Huang and Choi (2000) pointed out, the "alignment" problem is often not explicitly defined and apparently everyone understands what is and should be going on. They, however, adopted their own definition. In the current study, we take "word alignment" as the more viable task of "translation spotting", as in the ARCADE project.[1]

4.2 Our Approach

Our method is similar to Piperidis *et al.*'s as we share the observation that the source word and the target word should have similar frequencies if they are bilingual equivalence, except for function words. However, their method compares all source-target associations for every possible pair of words between the source sentence and the target sentence, and located the correct translation from the local maximum. We, on the other hand, adopt a simpler comparison, paying utmost attention to one term at a time.

Our approach starts with a sentence-aligned bilingual corpus. As said, bilingual corpora in the legal domain are relatively clean corpora. Sentences can often be one-to-one aligned. Given that legal terms are not always cross-lingually lexicalised in similar ways, as discussed in Section 3, term length and position in a sentence might not be reliable parameters for word alignment. Instead, we deal with one term at a time, taking all sentences containing the term into consideration; and we refer to the group of sentences containing a given term as "concordance lines" of that term. Thus within its

[1] http://www.up.univ-mrs.fr/~veronis/arcade/index-en.html

concordance lines, a given term often has higher frequency than other co-occurring words, except for function words. Since terms in legal texts are more likely to be consistently translated, translation equivalences in the target concordances should share a similar frequency with the source word. Hence, by analysing the frequency profiles, we can identify the words in the target language which are likely to be expressing the concept of the source word.

Our algorithm is as follows:

1. Extract salient compound terms from the word-segmented Chinese texts and treat them as single words in subsequent steps.
2. Mark up stop words from both the Chinese and English texts, and lemmatise the English words.
3. Scan through the Chinese texts. For each un-aligned word, retrieve all sentences containing the word to give the *source concordances*, and all corresponding, aligned sentences from the English texts to give the *target concordances*.
4. Perform a word frequency count from the concordances and rank the results.
5. Pick the words from target concordances above some frequency threshold. The longest string containing one or more of these words and spanning within a small window size in each target concordance gives a candidate of translation equivalence. (The setting of the threshold and the window size will be discussed in Section 5.2.)
6. Repeat Steps 3 to 5 until all Chinese words are processed.

Thus our method is not restricted to aligning single words. It does not inherently require a large corpus to start with. Also, no prior knowledge source like existing bilingual dictionaries is required.

5 Pilot Experiment

5.1 Test Materials

The corpus we used is a domain-specific one, consisting of parallel texts of Hong Kong court judgments, in English and Chinese.[2] Each judgment has a header containing the basic information of the case (e.g. case number, judges, etc.), the main judgment text, and a footer where judges sign. Only the main text was used in this experiment. For the current study, the Chinese texts contain about 200K characters, and about 113K word tokens and 7K word types upon segmentation. The parallel English texts contain about 120K word tokens, which correspond to about 7K word types. The corpus was aligned to the sentence level, and there were 4750 groups of aligned sentences.

5.2 Method

The algorithm proposed in Section 4.2 was applied to the sentence-aligned corpus. The sentence alignment was manually verified to ensure the idiosyncratic cases were rectified. The Chinese term extraction was done with the algorithm in Kwong and Tsou (2001). The English words were stemmed by applying the Porter (1980) stemmer. Only the Chinese terms occurring more than 5 times in the corpus were tackled. For the frequency threshold (in Step 5), we first look for words with frequency over $0.8 * source\ frequency$ (where *source frequency* is the frequency of the source term within the source concordances). If no words cross this threshold, we pick the word with the highest frequency and over $0.5 * source\ frequency$. For the window size, we took the empirically optimal $n + 1$ from Kwong (2002), where n is the number of English words crossing the frequency threshold.

5.3 Performance Measures

Alignment outcomes were classified into four types: *correct*, *partially correct*, *incorrect*, and *empty*, defined as follows:

- ***Correct***: All relevant content words are within the suggested translation equivalence, allowing incomplete verb forms or missing stop words before or after.
- ***Partially Correct***: Under- or over-aligned, with some content words outside or some irrelevant words inside the translation candidate.

[2]The authors acknowledge the Hong Kong Judiciary for providing the judgment texts.

- ***Incorrect***: Completely mis-aligned words.
- ***Empty***: No candidate translation equivalence is suggested.

5.4 Results

The Chinese term extraction yielded 683 potential compound terms (length ≥ 4 characters and without numerals), and 462 remained after human verification. Thus step 1 of the algorithm (see Section 4.2) re-segmented the Chinese texts with this list of compound terms.

As said earlier, the corpus contains 4750 aligned sentences. We evaluated the alignment of terms in 50 randomly selected sentences. Sentence lengths range from 2 to 45 Chinese words, and the average sentence length is 18.6 words.

Of the total 932 Chinese words in the 50 sentences, 359 were filtered as stop words, and 59 occurred five times or less. Hence, there were 514 words subject to alignment. The outcomes are summarised below.

Correct	=	213 (41%)
Partially Correct	=	19 (4%)
Incorrect	=	41 (8%)
Empty	=	241 (47%)

Considering all cases where a translation equivalence was suggested, our method attained 53% *coverage* and 85% *precision* (percentage of correct and partially correct equivalences among all suggested equivalences). The *recall* (percentage of correct and partially correct equivalences among all test instances) was 45%. Our method gives relatively high coverage and comparable precision, as compared to existing lexically based methods, which is especially encouraging in view of its knowledge independence.

Figure 1 shows an excerpt of the output. Words in the aligned sentences were numbered as seen at the top of Figure 1. Stop words and words with too few occurrences were not processed. The suggested alignment was listed after the whole Chinese sentence was processed. In the figure, for example, c6 was aligned to e4-e6. The resultant alignment of the sentence is drawn in Figure 2. In fact, we can find the various types of alignment outcomes in this example. The links (except the dotted one) indicate correct alignment. The dotted link for c14 is an incorrect match. There were no suggestions for c4, c5, c7, c8, and c10. Nevertheless, there were in fact no literal correspondences in the English sentence for c4, c7, c8, and c14. So some of the empty alignments are correct. Further classifying the empty outcomes and taking the correct ones into account, the accuracy of our method is over 55% as far as the word alignment per se is concerned. The results will be further analysed in the next section.

```
Sentence No. 4660
c1=他   c2=現在   c3=向   c4=法庭   c5=尋求
c6=上訴許可   c7=以便   c8=提出   c9=針對
c10=判罪   c11=及   c12=刑罰   c13=的   c14=上訴
e1=He   e2=now   e3=seeks   e4=leave   e5=to
e6=appeal   e7=against   e8=conviction   e9=and
e10=sentence
c1,他   (stop)
c2,現在,27
        1,now,20
c3,向   (stop)
c4,法庭,213
        1,court,160
c5,尋求,62
c6,上訴許可,17
        1,appeal,22
        2,leav,17
        3,applic,13
c7,以便,38
c8,提出,325
c9,針對,71
        1,against,57
c10,判罪,5   (too few)
c11,及   (stop)
c12,刑罰,49
        1,sentenc,50
c13,的   (stop)
c14,上訴,183
        1,appeal,226
Alignment:
c2:e2/!!c4:!!c5:!!c6:e4-e6/!!c7:!!c8:!!c9:e7/!!c10:!!c12:e10/!!c14:e6/!!
```

Figure 1: Excerpt of Alignment Output

As for the derivation of a translation lexicon, we thus obtained 213 suggested translation equivalences from the correct word alignments. These equivalences are potential entries of a bilingual legal term translation lexicon, upon further filtering and processing. Figure 3 shows some examples.

6 Discussion

In the last section, we have seen the effectiveness of our method from a pilot experiment. This finding is significant because the method overcomes the limitations of existing statisti-

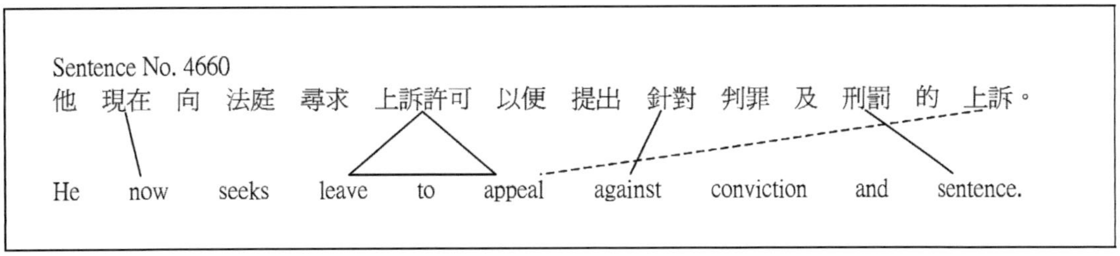

Figure 2: Graphical Representation of Resultant Alignment for Sentence 4660

cally based and lexically based methods. It does not depend on any prior knowledge source, and it works for a small, domain-specific, and parallel corpus of two very different languages. The method does not produce forced errors, and some empty alignments are actually correct. It is also able to align many personal names. In the following, we will further analyse the errors to explore ways for improving the algorithm.

As observed from the pilot test, alignment errors usually occurred for one or more of the following reasons:

- Errors are inherited from the term extraction step. There were some terms which should better be separated and some potential compound terms were not extracted by the algorithm. As a result, the frequency counts would be affected.
- General words may not be frequent enough to be successfully aligned. As court judgments also contain factual description as well as legal reasoning, the factual parts may contain more general words which are not as abundant as legal terms in the whole corpus.
- The method (and its current implementation) cannot distinguish multiple occurrences of the same term in a sentence, and the first occurrence will always be suggested. Word position may need to be taken as another parameter in the future. Moreover, the method now only suggests either one translation candidate or none. It should be fine-tuned to consider multiple candidates which might exist.
- Since the method takes the whole corpus to work out the frequency profiles, it means a given Chinese term would be aligned to its most frequently found translation in the corpus. If it happens that the term is expressed in a different (and less frequent) way in the target language in a particular pair of concordance, the method will result in an empty alignment, and thus missing translation equivalences.
- Anaphors also cause many alignment errors. Since pronouns are treated as stop words, if a term in the source language is pronominalised in the target language, there is no way to properly align that term.

Terms in Chinese	**English Equivalence**
上訴人	Appellant
普通法	Common law
強制執行	Enforcement
信納	Satisfied
書面查詢	Requisition
原訴人的律師	Plaintiff's solicitors
裁斷	Findings
舊式婚姻	Customary marriage

Figure 3: Examples of Acquired Translations

As the current study makes minimal use of syntactic information (e.g. no part-of-speech tagging was done and the compound terms extracted were not governed by any particular syntactic patterns), it might be useful to explore the contribution of some syntactic processing to the alignment performance and for solving some of the above problems.

Future work also includes the refinement of the acquired translation lexicon into one for legal terminology. This would require further processing of the translation equivalences suggested during the alignment process. For instance, entries in a lexicon should make sense even when out of context, so they should be free of anaphors like definite descriptions, and they should be in root form. Also, apart from filtering using a general dictionary as in Resnik and Melamed (1997), we may also filter the results against the terms found in a general-domain corpus.

7 Conclusion

In this study, we have introduced and tested a simple but effective method for word alignment and translation extraction between parallel English and Chinese legal texts, based on frequency profiles of parallel concordances. The method does not require any prior knowledge, and thus overcomes the limitations of existing statistically based and lexically based methods. It is especially designed for working with small, domain-specific, and sentence-aligned parallel corpora. About 85% precision and 45% recall were obtained from the pilot experiment. Future work will be on the fine-tuning of the algorithm and the acquired translation lexicon.

References

L. Borin. 2000. You'll take the high road and I'll take the low road: Using a third language to improve bilingual word alignment. In *Proceedings of the 18th International Conference on Computational Linguistics*, pages 97–103, Saarbrücken, Germany.

P. Fung. 1998. A statistical view on bilingual lexicon extraction: from parallel corpora to non-parallel corpora. *Lecture Notes in Artificial Intelligence*, 1529:1–17.

W.A. Gale and K.W. Church. 1991. A program for aligning sentences in bilingual corpora. In *Proceedings of the 29th Annual Conference of the Association for Computational Linguistics (ACL'91)*, pages 177–184, Berkeley, USA.

J-X. Huang and K-S. Choi. 2000. Chinese-Korean word alignment based on linguistic comparison. In *Proceedings of the 38th Annual Meeting of the Association for Computational Linguistics (ACL-2000)*, pages 392–399, Hong Kong.

M. Kay and M. Roescheisen. 1993. Text-translation alignment. *Computational Linguistics*, 19(1):121–142.

S.J. Ker and J.S. Chang. 1997. Aligning more words with high precision for small bilingual corpora. *Computational Linguistics and Chinese Language Processing*, 2(2):63–96.

O.Y. Kwong and B.K. Tsou. 2001. Automatic corpus-based extraction of Chinese legal terms. In *Proceedings of the 6th Natural Language Processing Pacific Rim Symposium (NLPRS 2001)*, pages 669–676, Tokyo, Japan.

O.Y. Kwong. 2002. Toward a bilingual legal term glossary from context profiles. In *Proceedings of the 16th Pacific Asia Conference on Language, Information and Computation (PACLIC 16)*, pages 249–258, Jeju, Korea.

G.S. Mann and D. Yarowsky. 2001. Multipath translation lexicon induction via bridge languages. In *Proceedings of the 2nd Meeting of the North American Chapter of the Association for Computational Linguistics (NAACL 2001)*, pages 151–158, Carnegie Mellon University, Pittsburgh, USA.

I.D. Melamed. 1997. A word-to-word model of translational equivalence. In *Proceedings of the 35th Conference of the Association for Computational Linguistics and 8th Conference of the European Chapter of the Association for Computational Linguistics (ACL/EACL'97)*, Madrid, Spain.

S. Piperidis, S. Boutsis, and I. Demiros. 1997. Automatic translation lexicon generation from multilingual texts. In *Proceedings of the 2nd Workshop on Multilinguality in Software Industry: The AI Contribution (MULSAIC'97)*, Nagoya, Japan.

M.F. Porter. 1980. An algorithm for suffix stripping. *Program*, 14(3):130–137, July.

P. Resnik and I.D. Melamed. 1997. Semi-automatic acquisition of domain-specific translation lexicons. In *Proceedings of the Fifth Conference on Applied Natural Language Processing (ANLP'97)*, Washington, DC.

M. Simard, G.F. Foster, and P. Isabelle. 1992. Using cognates to align sentences in bilingual corpora. In *Proceedings of the Fourth International Conference on Theoretical and Methodological Issues in Machine Translation (TMI-92)*, pages 67–81.

F.Z. Smadja, K. McKeown, and V. Hatzivassiloglou. 1996. Translating collocations for bilingual lexicons: A statistical approach. *Computational Linguistics*, 22(1):1–38.

D. Wu and X. Xia. 1995. Large-scale automatic extraction of an English-Chinese translation lexicon. *Machine Translation*, 9(3-4):285–313.

D. Wu. 1994. Aligning a parallel English-Chinese corpus statistically with lexical criteria. In *Proceedings of the 32nd Annual Meeting of the Association for Computational Linguistics (ACL-94)*, Las Cruces, NM.

Improving a general-purpose Statistical Translation Engine by Terminological lexicons

Philippe Langlais
RALI / DIRO / Université de Montréal
C.P. 6128, succursale Centre-ville
Montréal (Québec)
Canada, H3C 3J7
email:felipe@iro.umontreal.ca

Abstract

The past decade has witnessed exciting work in the field of Statistical Machine Translation (SMT). However, accurate evaluation of its potential in real-life contexts is still a questionable issue.

In this study, we investigate the behavior of an SMT engine faced with a corpus far different from the one it has been trained on. We show that terminological databases are obvious resources that should be used to boost the performance of a statistical engine. We propose and evaluate a way of integrating terminology into a SMT engine which yields a significant reduction in word error rate.

1 Introduction

SMT mainly became known to the linguistic community as a result of the seminal work of Brown et al. (1993b). Since then, many researchers have invested effort into designing better models than the ones proposed in the aforementioned article and several new exciting ways have been suggested to attack the problem.

For instance, Vogel et al. (1996) succeeded in overcoming the independence assumption made by IBM models by introducing order-1 Hidden Markov alignment models. Och et al. (1999) described an elegant way of integrating automatically acquired probabilistic templates into the translation process, and Nießen and Ney (2001) did the same for morphological information.

Radically different statistical models have also been proposed. (Foster, 2000) investigated maximum entropy models as an alternative to the so-called noisy-channel approach. Very recently, Yamada and Knight (2001) described a model in which the noisy-channel takes as input a parsed sentence rather than simple words.

While many of these studies include intensive evaluation sections, it is not always easy to determine exactly how well statistical translation can do on a given task. We know that on a specific task of spoken language translation, Wang (1998) provided evidence that SMT compared favorably to a symbolic translation system; but as mentioned by the author, the comparison was not totally fair.

We do not know of any studies that describe extensive experiments evaluating the adequacy of SMT in a real translation environment. We prefer not to commit ourselves to defining what a real translation task is; instead, we adopt the conservative point of view that a viable translation engine (statistical or not) is one that copes with texts that may be very different in nature from those used to train it.

This fairly general definition suggests that adaptativity is a cornerstone of a successful SMT engine. Curiously enough, we are not aware of much work on adaptative SMT, despite the tremendous amount of work done on adaptative statistical language modeling.

In this paper, we propose to evaluate how a statistical engine behaves when translating a very domain specific text which is far different from the corpus used to trained both our translation and language models. We first describe our translation engine. In section 3, we quantify and analyse the performance deterioration of an SMT engine trained on a broad-based corpus (the Hansard) when used to translate a domain specific text (in this study, a manual for military snipers). In section 4, We then suggest a simple but natural way of improving a broad-based SMT engine; that is, by opening the engine to available terminological resources. In section 5, we report on the improvement we observed by implementing our proposed approach. Finally, in section 6 we discuss other approaches we feel can lead to more robust translation.

2 Our statistical engine

2.1 The statistical models

In this study, we built an SMT engine designed to translate from French to English, following the noisy-channel paradigm first described by (Brown et al., 1993b). This engine is based on equation 1, where $e_1^{\hat{I}}$ stands for the sequence of $\hat{I}$ English target words to be found, given a French source sentence of J words f_1^J:

$$e_1^{\hat{I}} = \underset{I,e_1^I}{\text{argmax}} \ \underbrace{P(e_1^I)}_{\text{language}} \ . \ \underbrace{P(f_1^J|e_1^I)}_{\text{translation}} \qquad (1)$$

To train our statistical models, we assembled a bitext composed of 1.6 million pairs of sentences that were automatically aligned at the sentence level. In this experiment, every token was converted into lowercase before training.

The language model we used is an interpolated trigram we trained on the English sentences of our bitext. The perplexity of the resulting model is fairly low – 65 –, which actually reflects the fact that this corpus contains many fixed expressions (*e.g* `pursuant to standing order`).

The inverted translation model we used is an IBM2-like model: 10 iterations of IBM1-training were run (reducing the perplexity of the training corpus from 7776 to 90), followed by 10 iterations of IBM2-training (yielding a final perplexity of 54). We further reduced the number of transfer parameters (originally 34 969 331) by applying an algorithm described in Foster (2000); this algorithm basically filters in the pairs of words with the best gain, where gain is defined as the difference in perplexity — measured on a held-out corpus — of a model trained with this pair of words and a model trained without. In this experiment, we worked with a model containing exactly the first gain-ranked million parameters. It is interesting to note that by doing this, we not only save memory, and therefore time, but also obtain improvments in terms of perplexity and overall performance[1].

[1]On a translation task from French to English on Hansard sentences, we observed a reduction in word error rate of more than 3% with the reduced model.

2.2 The search algorithm

The maximum operation in equation 1, also called search or decoding, involves a length model. We assume that the length (counted in words) of French sentences that translate an English sentence of a given length follow a normal distribution.

We extended the decoder described by Nießen et al. (1998) to a trigram language model. The basic idea of this search algorithm is to expand hypotheses along the positions of the target string while progressively covering the source ones. We refer the reader to the original paper for the recursion on which it relies, and instead give in Figure 1 a sketch of how a translation is built. An hypothesis h is fully determined by four parameters: its source (j) and target (i) positions of the last word (e), and its coverage (c). Therefore, the search space can be represented as a 4-dimension table, each item of which contains backtracking information (f for the fertility of e, b_j and b_w for the source position and the target word we should look at to backtrack) and the hypothesis score ($prob$).

We know that better alignment models have been proposed and extensively compared (Och and Ney, 2000). We must however point out that the performance we obtained on the HANSARD corpus (see Section 3) is comparable to the rates published elsewhere on the same kind of corpus. In any case, our goal in this study is to compare the behavior of a SMT engine in both friendly and adverse situations. In our view, the present SMT engine is suitable for such a comparative study.

2.3 Tuning the decoder

The decoder has been tuned in several ways in order to reduce its computations without detrimentally affecting the quality of its output. The first thing we do when the decoder receives a sentence is to compute what we call an *active vocabulary*; that is, a collection of words which are likely to occur in the translation. This is done by ranking for each source word the target words according to their non normalized posterior likelihood (that is $\text{argmax}_e\, p(f|e)p(e)$, where $p(e)$ is given by a unigram target language model, and $p(f|e)$ is given by the transfer

Input: $f_1 \dots f_j \dots f_J$

Initialize the search space table *Space*
Select a maximum target length: I_{max}
Compute the active vocabulary

```
// Fill the search table recursively:
for all target position i = 1, 2, ..., I_max do
  prune(i − 1);
  for all alive hyp. h = Space(i, j, c, e) do
    uv ← History(h);
    zones ← FreeSrcPositions(h);
    bestWords ← NBestTgtWords(uv);
    for all w in bestWords do
      prob ← Score(h) + log p(w|uv);
      setIfBetter(i, j, c, b, prob, 0, j, v);
      for all free source position d do
        s ← prob;
        for all f ∈ [1, f_max] / d + f − 1 is
        free do
          s+ = log a(i|d, J) + log t(f_d|e_i);
          setIfBetter(i, d, c+f, w, s, f, j, w);

// Find and return the best hypothesis if any
max_s ← −∞
for all i ∈ [1, I_max] do
  for all alive hyp. h = Space(i, j, c, e) do
    s ← Score(h) + log p(i|J);
    if ((c == J) and (s > max_s)) then
      max_s ← s
      ⟨max_i, max_j, max_e⟩ ← ⟨i, j, e⟩
if (max_s! = ∞) then
  Return Space(max_i, max_j, J, max_e);
else
  Failure
```

Output: $e_1 \dots e_i \dots e_{max_i}$

Figure 1: Sketch of our decoder. *FreeSrcPositions* returns the source positions not already associated to words of h; *NBestTgtWords* returns the list of words that are likely to follow the last bigram uv preceeding e according to the language model; and $setIfBetter(i, j, c, e, p, f, b_j, b_w)$ is an operator that memorizes an hypothesis if its score (p) is greater than the hypothesis already stored in $Space(i, j, c, e)$. a and t stands for the alignment and transfert distributions used by IBM2 models.

probabilities of our inverted translation model) and keeping for each source word at most a target words.

Increasing a raises the coverage of the active vocabulary, but also slows down the translation process and increases the risk of admitting a word that has nothing to do with the translation. We have conducted experiments with various a-values, and found that an a-value of 10 offers a good compromise.

As mentioned in the block diagram, we also prune the space to make the search tractable. This is done with relative filtering as well as absolute thresholding. The details of all the filtering strategies we implemented are however not relevant to the present study.

3 Performances of our SMT engine

3.1 Test corpora

In this section we provide a comparison of the translation performances we measured on two corpora. The first one (namely, the HANSARD) is a collection of sentences extracted from a part of the Hansard corpus we did not use for training. In particular, we did not use any specific strategy to select these sentences so that they would be closely related to the ones that were used for training.

Our second corpus (here called SNIPER) is an excerpt of an army manual on sniper training and deployment that was used in an EARLIER study (Macklovitch, 1995). This corpus is highly specific to the military domain and would certainly prove difficult for any translation engine not specifically tuned to such material.

3.2 Overall performance

In this section, we evaluate the performance of our engine in terms of sentence- and word- error rates according to an oracle translation[2]. The first rate is the percentage of sentences for which the decoder found the exact translation (that is, the one of our oracle), and the word error rate is computed by a Levenstein distance (counting the same penalty for both *insertion*, *deletion* and *substitution* edition operations). We realize that these measures alone are not sufficient for a serious evaluation, but we were re-

[2]Both corpora have been published in both French and English, and we took the English part as the gold standard.

luctant in this experiment to resort to manual judgments, following for instance the protocol described in (Wang, 1998). Actually a quick look at the degradation in performance we observed on SNIPER is so clear that we feel these two rates are informative enough !

Table 1 summarizes the performance rates we measured. The WER is close to 60% on the HANSARD corpus and close to 74% on SNIPER; source sentences in the latter corpus being slightly longer on average (21 words). Not a single sentence was found to be identical to the gold standard translation on the SNIPER corpus [3].

corpus	*nbs*	$\vert length\vert$	SER	WER
HANSARD	1038	$\langle 16.2, 7.8\rangle$	95.6	59.6
SNIPER	203	$\langle 20.8, 6.8\rangle$	100	74.6

Table 1: Main characteristics of our test corpora and global performance of our statistical translator without any adjustments. $|length|$ reports the average length (counted in words) of the source sentences and the standard deviation; *nbs* is the number of sentences in the corpus.

3.3 Analyzing the performance drop

As expected, the poor performance observed on the SNIPER text is mainly due to two reasons: the presence of out of vocabulary (OOV) words and the incorrect translations of terminological units.

In the SNIPER corpus, 3.5% of the source tokens and 6.5% of the target ones are unknown to the statistical models. 44% of the source sentences and 77% of the target sentences contain at least one unknown word. In the HANSARD text, the OOV rates are much lower: around 0.5% of the source and target tokens are unknown and close to 5% of the source and target sentences contain at least one OOV words.

These OOV rates have a clear impact on the coverage of our active vocabulary. On the SNIPER text, 72% of the oracle tokens are in the active vocabulary (only 0.5% of the target sentences are fully covered); whilst on HANSARD, 86% of the oracle's tokens are covered (24% of the target sentences are fully covered).

Another source of disturbance is the presence of terminological units (TU) within the text to translate. Table 2 provides some examples of mistranslated TU from the SNIPER text. We also observed that many words within terminological units are not even known by the statistical models. Therefore accounting for terminology is one of the ways that should be considered to reduce the impact of OOV words.

< source term / oracle / translation>
<âme / bore / heart>
<huile polyvalente / general purpose oil / oil polyvalente>
<chambre / chamber / house of common>
<tireur d' élite / sniper / issuer of elite>
<la longueur de la crosse / butt length / the length of the crosse>

Table 2: Examples of mistranslated terminological entries of the SNIPER corpus.

4 Integrating non-probabilistic terminological resources

Using terminological resources to improve the quality of an automatic translation engine is not at all a new idea. However, we know of very few studies that actually investigated this avenue in the field of statistical machine translation. Among them, (Brown et al., 1993a) have proposed a way to exploit bilingual dictionnaries at training time. There may also be cases where domain-specific corpora are available which allow for the training of specialized models that can be combined with the general ones.

Another approach that would not require such material at training time consists in designing an adaptative translation engine. For instance, a cache-based language model could be used instead of our static trigram model. However, the design of a truly adaptative translation model remains a more speculative enterprise. At the very least, it would require a fairly precise location of errors in previously translated sentences; and we know from the ARCADE campaign on bilingual alignments, that accurate word alignments are difficult to obtain (Véronis and Langlais, 2000). This may be even more difficult in situations where errors will in-

[3] The full output of our translation sessions is available at `www-iro.umontreal.ca/~felipe/ResearchOutput/Computerm2002`

volve OOV words.

We investigated a third option, which involves taking advantage – at run time – of existing terminological resources, such as *Termium*[4]. As mentioned by Langlais et al. (2001), one of a translator's first tasks is often terminological research; and many translation companies employ specialized terminologists. Actually, aside from the infrequent cases where, in a given thematic context, a word is likely to have a clearly preferred translation (*e.g.* `bill`/*facture* *vs* `bill`/*projet de loi*), lexicons are often the only means for a user to influence the translation engine.

Merging such lexicons at run time offers a complementary solution to those mentioned above and it should be a fruitful strategy in situations where terminological resources are not available at training time (which may often be the case). Unfortunately, integrating terminological (or user) lexicons into a probabilistic engine is not a straightforward operation, since we cannot expect them to come with attached probabilities. Several strategies do come to mind, however. For instance, we could credit a translation of a sentence that contains a source lexicon entry in cases it contains an authorized translation. But this strategy may prouve difficult to tune since decoding usually involves many filtering strategies.

The approach we adopted consists in viewing a terminological lexicon as a set of constraints that are employed to reduce the search space. For instance, knowing that `sniper` is a sanctioned translation of *tireur d'élite*, we may require that current hypotheses in the search space associate the target word `sniper` with the three source French words.

In our implementation, we had to slightly modify the block diagram of Figure 1 in order to: 1) forbid a given word e_i from being associated with a word belonging to a source terminological unit, if it is not sanctioned by the lexicon; and 2) add at any target position an hypothesis linking a target lexicon entry to its source counterpart. Whether these hypotheses will survive intact will depend on constraints imposed by the maximum operation (of equation 1) over the full translation.

The score associated with a target entry $e_i^{i'}$ when linked to its source counterpart $f_j^{j'}$ in the latter case is given by:

$$\sum_{k\in[i,i']} \log p(e_k|e_{k-2}e_{k-1}) + \max_{l\in[j,j']} \log(a(k|l,J))$$

The rationale behind this equation is that both the language (p) and the alignment (a) models have some information that can help to decide the appropriateness of an extension: the former knows how likely it is that a word (known or not) will follow the current history[5]; and the latter knows to some extent where the target unit should be (regardless of its identity). In the absence of a better mechanism (e.g. a cache-model should be worth a try) We hope that this will be sufficient to determine the final position of the target unit in a given hypothesis.

5 Results

We considered three terminological lexicons whose characteristics are summarized in Table 3; they essentially differ in terms of number of entries and therefore coverage of the text to translate.

lexicon	nb	coverage	SER	WER
`sniper-1`	33	20/247	99	67.4
`sniper-2`	59	47/299	98	66.2
`sniper-3`	146	132/456	98	64.3

Table 3: Translation performance with different terminological lexicons. *nb* is the number of entries in the lexicon and *coverage* reports the number of different source entries from the lexicon belonging to the text to translate and the total number of their occurrences.

The first lexicon (namely `sniper-1`) contains the 33 entries used in the study of terminological consistency checking described in (Macklovitch, 1995). The second and third lexicons (namely `sniper-2` and `sniper-3`) contain those entries plus other ones added manually after an incremental inspection of the SNIPER corpus.

As can be observed from Table 3, introducing terminological lexicons into the translation engine does improve performance, measured in terms of WER, and this even with lexicons that

[4] See `http://www.termium.com/site/`.

[5] Our trigram model has been trained to provide parameters such as $p(UNK|ab)$.

Source	le **tireur d' élite** voit simultanément les **fils croisés** et l' image (l' objectif) .
Target	the **sniper** sees the **crosshairs** and the image - target - at the same time .
without	*the gunman being same son sit and picture of the hon. members : agreed .*
with	*the **sniper** simultaneously see the **crosshairs** and the image (objective .)*
Source	contrôle de la **détente** .
Target	exercising **trigger** control .
without	*the control of détente .*
with	*control of the **trigger** .*

Table 4: Two examples of translation *with* and *without* a terminological lexicon; TU appear in bold.

cover only a small portion of the text to translate. With the narrow coverage lexicon, we observe an absolute reduction of 7%, and a reduction of 10% with the broader lexicon `sniper-3`. This suggests that adding more entries into the lexicon is likely to decrease WER. In another study (Carl and Langlais, 2002), we investigated whether an automatic procedure designed to detect term variants could improve these performances futher.

Table 4 provides two examples of translation outputs, with and without the help of terminological units. The first one clearly shows that EVEN A few TU (two in this case) may substantially improve the quality of the translation output; (the translation produced without the lexicon was particularly poor in this very case.

Even though terminological lexicons do improve the overall WER figure, a systematic inspection of the outputs produced with TU reveals that the translations are still less faithful to the source text than the translations produced for the HANSARD text. OOV words remain a serious problem.

6 Discussion

In this study, we have shown that translating texts in specific domains with a general[-]purpose statistical engine is difficult. This suggests the need to implementing an adaptative strategy. Among the possible scenarios, we have shown that opening the engine to terminological resources is a natural and efficient way of softening the decoder.

In a similar vein, Marcu (2001) investigated how to combine Example Based Machine Translation (EBMT) and SMT approaches. The author automatically derived from the Hansard corpus what he calls a translation memory: actually a collection of pairs of source and target word sequences that are in a translation relation according to the viterbi alignment run with an IBM4 model that was also trained on the Hansard corpus. This collection of phrases was then merged with a greedy statistical decoder to improve the overall performance of the system.

What this study suggests is that translation memories collected from a given corpus can improve the performance of a statistical engine trained on the same corpus, which in itself is an interesting result. A very similar study but with weaker results is derscribed in (Langlais et al., 2000), in the framework of the TRANSTYPE project. Besides the different metrics the authors used, the discrepancy in performance in these two studies may be explained by the nature of the test corpora used. The test corpus in the latter study was more representative of a real translation task, while the test corpus that Marcu used was a set of around 500 French sentences of no more than 10 words.

Our present study is close in spirit to these last two, except that we do not attack the problem of automatically acquiring bilingual lexicons; instead, we consider it a part of the translator's task to provide such lexicons. Actually, we feel this may be one of the only ways a user has of retaining some control over the engine's output, a fact that professional translators seem to appreciate (Langlais et al., 2001).

As a final remark, we want to stress that we see the present study as a first step toward the eventual unification of EBMT and SMT, and in this respect we agree with (Marcu, 2001). Potentially, of course, EBMT can offer much more than just a simple list of equivalences, like those we used in this study. However, the basic approach we describe here still holds, as long as we can extend the notion of *constraint* used in this study to include non-consecutive sequences of words. This is a problem we we plan to investigate in future research.

Acknowledgments

I am indebted to Elliott Macklovitch and George Foster for the fruitful orientation they gave to this work.

References

Peter F. Brown, Stephen A. Della Pietra, Vincent J. Della Pietra, Meredith J. Goldsmith, Jan Hajic, Robert L. Mercer, and Surya Mohanty. 1993a. But dictionaries are data too. In *Human Language Technology (HLT)*, pages 202–205, Princeton, NJ, march.

Peter F. Brown, Stephen A. Della Pietra, Vincent J. Della Pietra, and Robert L. Mercer. 1993b. The mathematics of statistical machine translation: Parameter estimation. *Computational Linguistics*, 19(2):263–311.

Michael Carl and Philippe Langlais. 2002. Toward an intelligent terminology database as a front-and backend for statistical machine translation. In *COMPUTERM 2002*, Taipei.

George Foster. 2000. A Maximum Entropy / Minimum Divergence translation model. In *Proceedings of the 38th Annual Meeting of the ACL*, pages 37–44, Hong Kong, October.

Philippe Langlais, George Foster, and Guy Lapalme. 2000. Unit completion for a computer-aided translation typing system. In *Proceedings of the 5th Conference on Applied Natural Language Processing (ANLP)*, pages 135–141, Seattle, Washington, May.

Philippe Langlais, George Foster, and Guy Lapalme. 2001. Integrating bilingual lexicons in a probabilistic translation assistant. In *Proceedings of the 8th Machine Translation Summit*, pages 197–202, Santiago de Compostela, Galicia, Spain, September. IAMT.

Elliott Macklovitch. 1995. Can terminological consistency be validated automatically ? Technical report, CITI/RALI, Montréal, Canada.

Daniel Marcu. 2001. Towards a unified approach to memory- and statistical-based machine translation. In *Proceedings of the 39th Annual Meeting of the ACL*, pages 378–385, Toulouse, France.

Sonja Nießen and Hermann Ney. 2001. Toward hierarchical models for statistical machine translation of inflected languages. In *Proceedings of the Workshop on Data Driven Machine Translation yielded at the 39th Annual Meeting of the ACL*, pages 47–54, Toulouse, France.

Sonja Nießen, Stephan Vogel, Hermann Ney, and Christoph Tillmann. 1998. A dp based search algorithm for statistical machine translation. In *Proceedings of the 36th Annual Meeting of the ACL and the 17th COLING*, pages 960–966, Montréal, Canada, August.

Franz Joseph Och and Hermann Ney. 2000. A comparison of alignement models for statistical machine translation. In *Proceedings of the International Conference on Computational Linguistics (COLING) 2000*, pages 1086–1090, Saarbrucken, Luxembourg, Nancy, August.

Franz Josef Och, Christoph Tillman, and Herman Ney. 1999. Improved alignment models for statistical machine translation. In *Proceedings of the 4nd Conference on Empirical Methods in Natural Language Processing (EMNLP)*, pages 20–28, College Park, Maryland.

Jean Véronis and Philippe Langlais, 2000. *Evaluation of parallel text alignment systems: The ARCADE project*, volume 13, chapter 19, pages 369–388. Parallel Text Processing, Kluwer.

Stephan Vogel, Hermann Ney, and Christoph Tillmann. 1996. Hmm-based word alignement in statistical translation. In *Proceedings of the International Conference on Computational Linguistics (COLING) 1996*, pages 836–841, Copenhagen, Denmark, August.

Ye-Yi Wang. 1998. *Grammar Inference and Statistical Machine Translation.* Ph.D. thesis, CMU-LTI, Carnegie Mellon University.

Kenji Yamada and Kevin Knight. 2001. A syntax-based statistical translation model. In *Proceedings of the 39th Annual Meeting of the ACL*, pages 531–538, Toulouse, France.

Probabilistic named entity verification

Yi-Chung Lin and Peng-Hsiang Hung
Advanced Technology Center, Computer and Communications Laboratories,
Industrial Technology Research Institute, Taiwan
{lyc,phhung}@itri.org.tw

Abstract

Named entity (NE) recognition is an important task for many natural language applications, such as Internet search engines, document indexing, information extraction and machine translation. Moreover, in oriental languages (such as Chinese, Japanese and Korean), NE recognition is even more important because it significantly affects the performance of word segmentation, the most fundamental task for understanding the texts in oriental languages. In this paper, a probabilistic verification model is designed for verifying the correctness of a named entity candidate. This model assesses the confidence level of a candidate not only according to the candidate's structure but also according to its context. In our design, the clues for confidence measurement are collected from both positive and negative examples in the training data in a statistical manner. Experimental results show that the proposed method significantly improves the F-measure of Chinese personal name recognition from 86.5% to 94.4%.

Introduction

Named entity (NE) recognition (or proper name recognition) is a task to find the entities of person, location, organization, date, time, percentage and monetary value in text documents. It is an important task for many natural language applications, such as Internet search engines, document indexing, information extraction and machine translation. Moreover, in oriental languages (such as Chinese, Japanese and Korean), NE recognition is even more important because it significantly affects the performance of word segmentation, the most fundamental task for understanding the texts in oriental languages. Therefore, a high-accuracy NE recognition method is highly demanded for most natural language applications in various languages.

There are two major approaches to NE recognition: the handcrafted approach (Grishman, 1995) and the statistical approach (Bikel, 1997; Chen, 1998; Yu, 1998). In the first approach, a system usually relies on a large number of handcrafted rules. This kind of systems can be rapid prototyped but are hard to scale up. In fact, there will be numerous exceptions for most handcrafted rules. It is generally expensive and impossible to code for every exception we can imagine, not to mention those exceptions we are not able to think of. Another serious problem with the handcrafted approach is that systems are hard to be ported across different domains and different languages. Porting a handcrafted system usually means rewriting all its rules. Therefore, the statistical approach is becoming more and more popular because of its cost-effectiveness in scaling up and porting systems.

In general, the statistical approach to NE recognition can be viewed as a two-stage process. First, according to dictionaries and/or pattern matching rules, the input text is tokenized into tokens. Each token may be a word or an NE candidate which can consist of more than one word. Then, the most likely token sequence is selected according to a statistical model, such as Markov model (Bikel, 1997; Yu, 1998) or maximum entropy model (Borthwick, 1999). Although, the statistical NE recognition is much more scalable and portable, its performance is still not satisfactory. The insufficient coverage/precision of pattern matching rules and unknown words are the major sources of errors. Furthermore, the role of the statistical model is to assess the relative possibilities of all possible token sequences and select the most probable one. The scores obtained from the statistical model can be used for a comparison of competing token sequences, but not for an assessment of the probability that a spotted named entity is correct.

To reduce the recognition errors, we propose a probabilistic verification model to verify the correctness of a named entity. This model assesses the confidence level of a named entity candidate not only according to the candidate's structure but also according to its contexts. In our design, the clues for confidence measurement are collected from both positive and negative examples in the training data. Therefore, the confidence measure has strong discriminant power for judging the correctness of a named entity. In the experiments of Chinese personal name recognition, the proposed verification model increases the F-measure from 86.5% to 94.4%, which corresponds to 58.5% error reduction rate, where "error rate" is defined as "100% – F-measure".

1. Named Entity Verification

As mentioned before, there are several kinds of named entities, including person, location, organization, date, time, percentage and monetary value. In the following description, we use the task of verifying Chinese personal name as an example. However, our proposed method is also applicable on verifying other kinds of named entities in different languages.

Before introducing our approach, we first describe the notations that will be used. In this proposal, a random variable is written with a boldface italic letter. An outcome of a random variable is written with the same italic letter but in normal face. For example, an outcome of the random variable $\boldsymbol{o}$ is denoted as o. If there is no confusion, we usually use $P(o)$ to denote the probability $P(\boldsymbol{o}=o)$. A symbol sequence "$x_1,\cdots,x_n$" is denoted as "x_1^n". Likewise, "$x_{Y,1}^{Y,n}$" denotes the sequence "$x_{Y,1},\cdots,x_{Y,n}$".

The task of verifying a named entity candidate is viewed as making an acceptance or rejection decision according to the text segment consisting of the candidate and its context. Without loss of generality, a text segment is

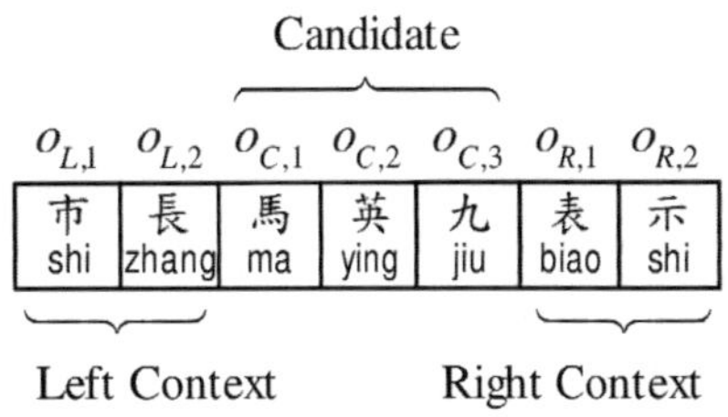

Figure 1: Example of a text segment.

considered as an outcome of the random vector $\boldsymbol{O}=[\boldsymbol{o}_{L,1}^{L,x},\boldsymbol{o}_{C,1}^{C,y},\boldsymbol{o}_{R,1}^{R,z}]$. The outcome of each random variable in $\boldsymbol{O}$ is one basic element of text. In Chinese, the basic elements of text are Chinese characters. However, in English, the basic elements are English words. Figure 1 shows an example of a text segment in which the size of the candidate to be verified is 3 (i.e., consists of three Chinese characters) and the sizes of its left context and right context are set to 2 (i.e., two Chinese characters).

Figure 2 depicts the flowchart of our verification approach. First, the candidate in the input text segment is parsed by a predefined grammar. If the candidate is ill-formed (i.e., fail

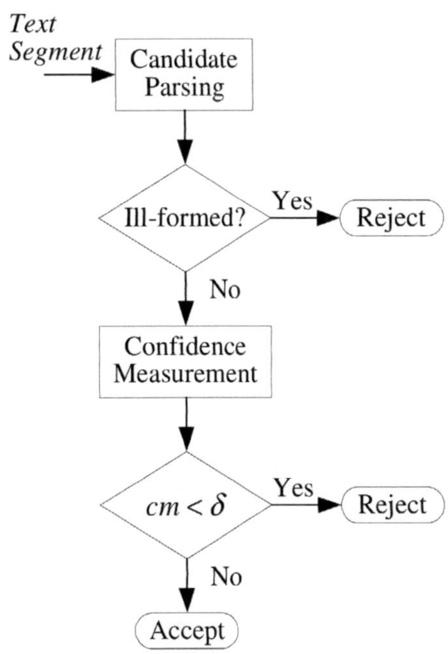

Figure 2: Flowchart of the verification method.

to be parsed), it will be rejected immediately. Otherwise, the text segment is passed to the confidence measurement module to assess the confidence level that the candidate in the text segment is to be a named entity. If the confidence measure is less than a predefined threshold, the candidate will be rejected. Otherwise, it will be accepted.

2. Confidence Measurement

The basic idea of our approach is to formulate the confidence measurement problem as the problem of hypothesis testing. The null hypothesis H_0 in which the candidate is a name is tested against the alternative hypothesis H_1 in which the candidate is not a name. According to Neyman-Pearson Lemma, an optimal hypothesis test involves the evaluation of the following log likelihood ratio:

$$\begin{aligned} &LLR(o_{L,1}^{L,x}, o_{C,1}^{C,y}, o_{R,1}^{R,z}) \\ &= \log \frac{P(o_{L,1}^{L,x}, o_{C,1}^{C,y}, o_{R,1}^{R,z} \mid H_0)}{P(o_{L,1}^{L,x}, o_{C,1}^{C,y}, o_{R,1}^{R,z} \mid H_1)} \\ &= \log P(o_{L,1}^{L,x}, o_{C,1}^{C,y}, o_{R,1}^{R,z} \mid H_0) \\ &\quad - \log P(o_{L,1}^{L,x}, o_{C,1}^{C,y}, o_{R,1}^{R,z} \mid H_1) \end{aligned} \quad (1)$$

where $P(o_{L,1}^{L,x}, o_{C,1}^{C,y}, o_{R,1}^{R,z} \mid H_0)$ is the likelihood of the candidate and its left and right contexts given the hypothesis that the candidate is a name and $P(o_{L,1}^{L,x}, o_{C,1}^{C,y}, o_{R,1}^{R,z} \mid H_1)$ is the likelihood of the candidate and its left and right contexts given the hypothesis that the candidate is not a name. The hypothesis test is performed by comparing the log likelihood ratio $LLR(o_{L,1}^{L,x}, o_{C,1}^{C,y}, o_{R,1}^{R,z})$ to a predefined critical

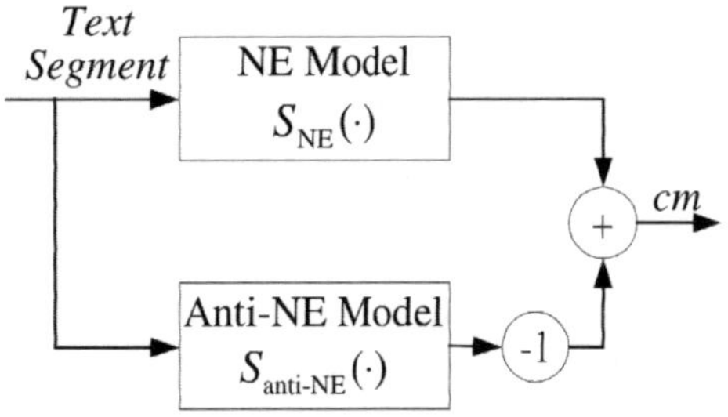

Figure 3: Block diagram of the confidence measurement module.

threshold δ. If $LLR(o_{L,1}^{L,x}, o_{C,1}^{C,y}, o_{R,1}^{R,z}) \geq \delta$, the null hypothesis will be accepted. Otherwise, it will be rejected.

In our design, as shown in Figure 3, the confidence measurement module consists of two models, named NE model and anti-NE model. The NE model is used to assess the value of $\log P(o_{L,1}^{L,x}, o_{C,1}^{C,y}, o_{R,1}^{R,z} \mid H_0)$ and the anti-NE model is used to assess the value of $\log P(o_{L,1}^{L,x}, o_{C,1}^{C,y}, o_{R,1}^{R,z} \mid H_1)$.

2.1. NE Model

The purpose of the NE model is to evaluate the value of $\log P(o_{L,1}^{L,x}, o_{C,1}^{C,y}, o_{R,1}^{R,z} \mid H_0)$, the log likelihood of the candidate and its left and right contexts given the hypothesis that the candidate is a name. Since it is infeasible to directly estimate the probability $P(o_{L,1}^{L,x}, o_{C,1}^{C,y}, o_{R,1}^{R,z} \mid H_0)$, it is approximated as follows:

$$\begin{aligned} &P(o_{L,1}^{L,x}, o_{C,1}^{C,y}, o_{R,1}^{R,z} \mid H_0) \equiv P_0(o_{L,1}^{L,x}, o_{C,1}^{C,y}, o_{R,1}^{R,z}) \\ &\approx P_0(o_{L,1}^{L,x}) P_0(o_{C,1}^{C,y}) P_0(o_{R,1}^{R,z}) \end{aligned} \quad (2)$$

where the subscript of $P_0(\cdot)$ indicates the probability is evaluated given that the null hypothesis is true. The probability $P_0(o_{L,1}^{L,x})$ is further approximated according to the bigram model as follows:

$$P_0(o_{L,1}^{L,x}) \approx \prod_{i=1}^{x} P_0(o_{L,i} \mid o_{L,i-1}) \quad (3)$$

where $P_0(o_{L,1} \mid o_{L,0}) \equiv P_0(o_{L,1})$. One should notice that we do not assume that the random sequence $\boldsymbol{o}_{L,1}^{L,x}$ is time invariant. For example, the probability $P(\boldsymbol{o}_{L,i} = x \mid \boldsymbol{o}_{L,i-1} = y)$ is not assumed to be equal to $P(\boldsymbol{o}_{L,2} = x \mid \boldsymbol{o}_{L,1} = y)$ for $i \geq 3$. Likewise, the probability $P_0(o_{R,1}^{R,z})$ is also further approximated as follows:

$$P_0(o_{R,1}^{R,z}) \approx \prod_{i=1}^{z} P_0(o_{R,i} \mid o_{R,i-1}) \quad (4)$$

where $P_0(o_{R,1} \mid o_{R,0}) \equiv P_0(o_{R,1})$.

The probability corresponding to the candidate is evaluated by applying the SCFG (Sto-

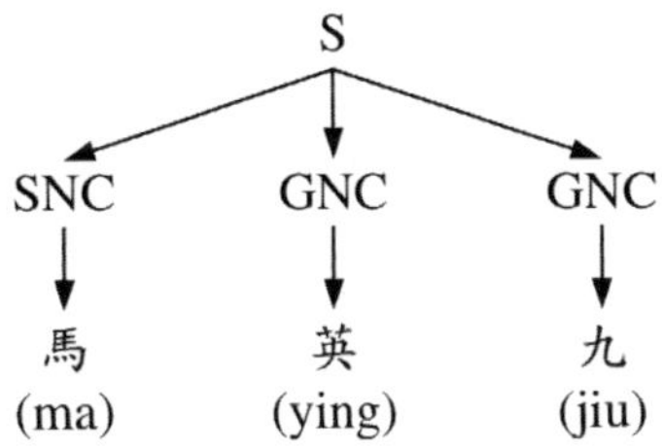

Figure 4: A parse tree of the Chinese personal name "馬英九(ma ying jiu)".

chastic Context-free Grammar) model (Fujisaki, 1989) as follows:

$$P_0(o_{C,1}^{C,y}) = \sum_T P_0(T) \approx \max_T P_0(T) = \max_T \prod_{A\to\alpha\in T} P_0(\alpha \mid A) \quad (5)$$

where T stands for one possible parse tree that derive the candidate, $A \to \alpha$ indicates a rule in the parse tree T, A stands for the left-hand-side symbol of the rule and α stands for the sequence of right-hand-side symbols of the rule. Figure 4 shows an example of a parse tree of the Chinese personal name candidate "馬英九(ma ying jiu)", where "馬(ma)" is the surname and "英九(ying jiu)" is the given name. In this figure, the symbol "S" denotes the start symbol, the symbol "SNG" denotes the nonterminal deriving surname characters and the symbol "GNC" denotes the nonterminal deriving given name characters. As a result, according to equations (2) -(5), the scoring function in the NE model is defined as equation (6) to assess the log likelihood of the text segment "$o_{L,1}^{L,x}, o_{C,1}^{C,y}, o_{R,1}^{R,z}$" given the null hypothesis that "$o_{C,1}^{C,y}$" is a name.

$$S_{\text{NE}}(o_{L,1}^{L,x}, o_{C,1}^{C,y}, o_{R,1}^{R,z}) = \sum_{i=1}^{x} \log P_0(o_{L,i} \mid o_{L,i-1}) + \sum_{i=1}^{z} \log P_0(o_{R,i} \mid o_{R,i-1}) + \max_T \sum_{A\to\alpha\in T} \log P_0(\alpha \mid A) \quad (6)$$

where T is one possible parse tree that derive the candidate "$o_{C,1}^{C,y}$".

2.2. Anti-NE Model

The purpose of the anti-NE model is to evaluate the value of $\log P(o_{L,1}^{L,x}, o_{C,1}^{C,y}, o_{R,1}^{R,z} \mid H_1)$, the log likelihood of the candidate and its left and right contexts given the hypothesis that the candidate is not a name. Since it is infeasible to directly estimate the probability $P(o_{L,1}^{L,x}, o_{C,1}^{C,y}, o_{R,1}^{R,z} \mid H_1)$, it is approximated as follows:

$$P(o_{L,1}^{L,x}, o_{C,1}^{C,y}, o_{R,1}^{R,z} \mid H_1) = P_1(o_{L,1}^{L,x}, o_{C,1}^{C,y}, o_{R,1}^{R,z}) \approx \prod_{i=1}^{x} P_1(o_{L,i} \mid o_{L,i-1}) \times \prod_{i=1}^{y} P_1(o_{C,i} \mid o_{C,i-1}) \times \prod_{i=1}^{z} P_1(o_{R,i} \mid o_{R,i-1}) \quad (7)$$

where $o_{R,0} \equiv o_{C,y}$, $o_{C,0} \equiv o_{L,x}$, and $P_1(o_{L,1} \mid o_{L,0}) \equiv P_1(o_{L,1})$. Therefore, the following scoring function is used in the anti-NE model to assess the log likelihood of the text segment "$o_{L,1}^{L,x}, o_{C,1}^{C,y}, o_{R,1}^{R,z}$" given the alternative hypothesis that "$o_{C,1}^{C,y}$" is not a name.

$$S_{\text{anti-NE}}(o_{L,1}^{L,x}, o_{C,1}^{C,y}, o_{R,1}^{R,z}) = \sum_{i=1}^{x} \log P_1(o_{L,i} \mid o_{L,i-1}) + \sum_{i=1}^{y} \log P_1(o_{C,i} \mid o_{C,i-1}) + \sum_{i=1}^{z} \log P_1(o_{R,i} \mid o_{R,i-1}) \quad (8)$$

3. Experiment Setup

The proposed named entity verification method is used to recognize Chinese personal names from news. In Chinese, most of the personal names consist of three Chinese characters. The first character is a surname. The last two characters are a given name. Therefore, our preliminary experiments are focused on recognizing the personal names of three Chinese characters.

In our experiments, the training corpus consists of about 14,339,000 Chinese characters collected from economy and industry news. This corpus should be annotated to estimate the probabilistic parameters of the scoring functions $S_{\text{NE}}(\cdot)$ and $S_{\text{anti-NE}}(\cdot)$. However, labeling such large amount of data is too costly or prohibited even if it is possible. Therefore, labeling

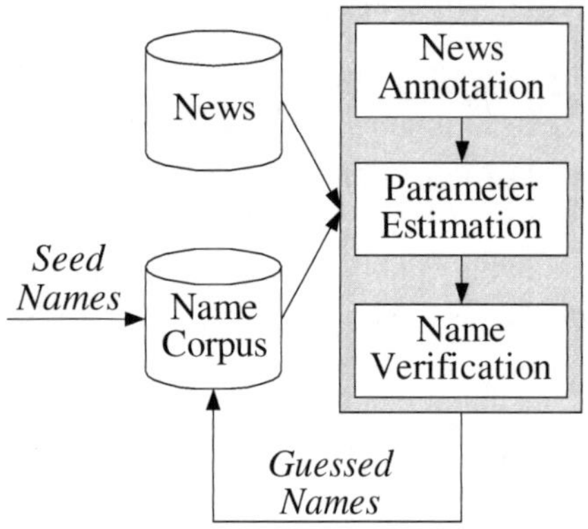

Figure 5: EM-style bootstrapping.

methods that can be bootstrapped from a little seed data or a few seed rules (Collins, 1999; Cucerzan, 1999) are highly demanded to automatically annotate the training data. In the following section, we propose an EM-style bootstrapping procedure (Cucerzan, 1999) for annotating the training data automatically.

3.1. EM-Style Bootstrapping

The Expectation-Maximization (EM) algorithm (Moon, 1996) has been widely used to estimate model parameters from incomplete data in many different applications. In this section, an EM-style bootstrapping procedure is proposed to automatically annotate the named entities in the training corpus. It iteratively uses the proposed verification model to label the training corpus (expectation step), and then uses the labeled training corpus to re-estimate the parameters of the verification model (maximization step). Figure 5 shows the flowchart of the bootstrapping procedure. First, we collect the names of 541 famous people, including government officers and CEOs of big companies. These names are used as seed names of the name corpus. Then, the news is automatically annotated according to the name corpus. The annotated corpus is used to estimate the probabilistic parameters of the scoring functions. Afterward, the proposed verification procedure is used to verify every possible name candidate in the news. The candidates whose confidence measures are larger than a predefined threshold are determined to be names. Currently, if the confidence measures of two overlapped candidates (such as "ma ying jiu" and "ying jiu biao" in Figure 1) pass the threshold, both of them are determined as names. Although this strategy is inadequate, it does not make too much trouble because the chance to get overlapped names is very small in our experiments. Finally, these guessed names are added to the name corpus which will be used to annotate the news in next iteration.

In our case, after four iterations, the size of name corpus is enlarged from 541 to 6,296, as shown in Table 1. The total occurrence frequency of these 6,296 names in the training corpus is 40,345.

3.2. Baseline Model

In the past, many researchers have studied the problem of Chinese personal name recognition. Chang (1994) used the 0-order Markov model to segment a text into words, including Chinese personal names. In his approach, a name probability model is proposed to estimate the probabilities of Chinese personal names. Sproat (1994) proposed to recognize Chinese personal names with the stochastic finite-state word segmentation algorithm. His approach is similar to Chang's, except that the name probability model is slightly different. In addition to name probability, Chen (1998) also add extra scores to a name candidate according to context clues (such as position, title, speech-act verbs). In the researches mentioned above, the reported F-measure performances on recognizing Chinese personal names are somewhere between 70% and 86%. Since these performances are meas-

Iteration	Nunber of distinct names	Total frequency of names
0	541	18310
1	3389	31157
2	5327	37423
3	6055	39977
4	6296	40345

Table 1: Number of distinct names in the name corpus and total frequency of names in the annotated news during the bootstrapping iteration.

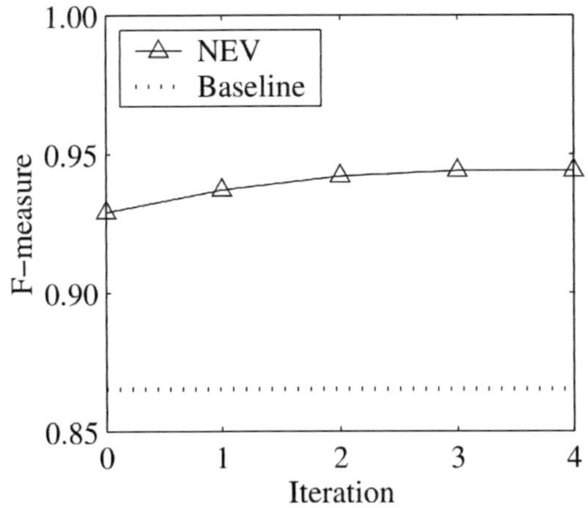

Figure 6: The performances of baseline and name entity verification (NEV).

ured based on different data, higher reported performance does not imply better. In fact, the name probability models used in these researches are very similar. Their performances should be comparable to each other. Therefore, in this paper, Chang's approach, whose reported F-measure is 86%, is chosen as the baseline model.

The baseline model is additionally equipped with a dictionary of 72,333 Chinese words. The prior probabilities of words are estimated from *Academia Sinica Balanced Corpus*, which contains about 2 million Chinese words.

4. Experimental Results and Discussions

Both the baseline model and the proposed name entity verification model (named NEV model) are tested on the same testing corpus. The testing corpus, also collected from economy and industry news, consists of about 737,000 characters. This corpus is annotated manually and contains totally 2,545 Chinese personal names.

The F-measure of the baseline model is 86.5% (as indicated by the dashed line in Figure 6). The precision and recall rates of the baseline model are 79.1% and 95.5% respectively. Although the recall rate of the baseline model is high, the precision rate is pretty low. Over 20% of the name candidates proposed by the baseline model are incorrect.

In our experiments, the sizes of the left- and right-context windows of the NEV model are set to 2. In Figure 6, the solid line with triangle markers depicts the F-measure of the NEV model versus the iteration number of bootstrapping. The F-measure saturates after 3 iterations. After 4 iterations, the F-measure of the NEV model reaches 94.4%. The corresponding precision and recall rates are 96.4% and 92.5% respectively. Compared with the baseline model, the precision rate is greatly improved from 79.1% to 96.4% with a little sacrifice in recall rate. The F-measure is improved from 86.5% to 94.4%, which corresponds to 58.5% error reduction rate, where "error rate" is defined as "100% – F-measure".

Table 2 lists three examples of the misrecognized names made by the baseline model. These examples clearly show that the baseline model tends to incorrectly group consecutive single characters, either from unknown words or single-character words, into names. In the first two examples, the single characters come from the unknown location name "卡羅來納(ga luo lai na; *Carolina*) and the unknown company name "羅技(luo ji; *Logitech*)". The single characters in the last example are single-character words "季(gi; *quarter*)", "全(quan; *all*)" and "美(mei; *USA*)".

Without the inadequate strong tendency of grouping single characters, the NEV model is able to avoid the misrecognition errors made by the baseline model. The NEV model assesses the confidence measure of each name candidate according to the context around the candidate. In Table 2, the name candidates in the shaded boxes are rejected by the NEV model because

以 北 卡 **羅 來 納** 州 為 例 yi bei ga **luo lai na** zhou wei li *(take North Carolina State as an example)*
大 廠 **羅 技 在** 去 年 da chang **luo ji zai** qu nian ... *(In last year, the big company Logitech ...)*
第 一 **季 全 美** 勞 動 者 di yi **ji quan mei** lao dong zhe ... *(In the first quarter, the workers in all USA ...)*

Table 2: Examples of the incorrect Chinese personal names (in the shaded boxes) produced by the baseline model.

their confidence measures are too low.

To sum up, the experimental results demonstrate that the contextual information, either from positive examples or from negative examples, is very helpful for named entity verification. Besides, the superiority of the NEV model also shows that the proposed probabilistic score functions $S_{NE}(\cdot)$ and $S_{anti\text{-}NE}(\cdot)$ are effective in providing the scores to produce a reliable confidence measure. Especially, the proposed named entity verification approach does not require any dictionary in advance.

Conclusion

Named entity (NE) recognition is an important task for many natural language applications, such as Internet search engines, document indexing, information extraction and machine translation. Moreover, in oriental languages (such as Chinese, Japanese and Korean), NE recognition is even more important because it significantly affects the performance of word segmentation, the most fundamental task for understanding the texts in oriental languages.

In this paper, a probabilistic verification model is proposed to verify the correctness of a named entity. This model assesses the confidence level of a name candidate not only according to the candidate's structure but also according to its contexts. The clues for confidence measurement are collected from both positive and negative examples in the training data. Therefore, the confidence measure has strong discriminant power for judging the correctness of a named entity. In the experiments of Chinese personal name recognition, the proposed verification model greatly increases the precision rate from 79.1% to 96.4% with a little sacrifice in recall rate. The F-measure is improved from 86.5% to 94.4%, which corresponds to 58.5% error reduction rate, where "error rate" is defined as "100% – F-measure".

Acknowledgements

This paper is a partial result of Project A311XS1211 conducted by ITRI under sponsorship of the Ministry of Economic Affairs, R.O.C. Especially thanks to the CKIP group of Academia Sinica for providing the *Academia Sinica Balanced Corpus*.

References

Bikel, D., Miller S., Schwartz R., and Weischedel R. (1997) *Nymble: A High-performance Learning Name Finder.* In Proceedings of the Fifth Conference on Applied Natural Language Processing, pp. 194–201.

Borthwick, A. (1999) *A Maximum Entropy Approach to Named Entity Recognition.* Ph.D. Thesis, New York University.

Chang J., Chen S., Ker S., Chen Y. and Liu J. (1994) *A Multiple-Corpus Approach to Recognition of Proper Names in Chinese Texts.* Computer Processing of Chinese and Oriental Languages, Vol. 8, No. 1, pp. 75-85.

Chen, H., Ding Y., Tsai S. and Bian G. (1998) *Description of the NTU System used for MET2.* in Proceedings of the 7th Message Understanding Conference (MUC-7)

Collins, M. and Singer, Y. (1999) *Unsupervised Models for Named Entity Classification.* In Proceedings of the Joint SIGDAT Conference on Empirical Methods in Natural Language Processing and Very Large Corpora, pp. 100-110.

Cucerzan S. and Yarowsky D. (1999) *Language independent named entity recognition combining morphological and contextual evidence.* In Proceedings of the Joint SIGDAT Conference on Empirical Methods in Natural Language Processing and Very Large Corpora, pp. 90-99.

Fujisaki, T., Jelinek F., Cocke J., Black E. and Nishino T. (1989), *A Probabilistic Parsing Method for Sentence Disambiguation.* In Proceedings of the International Workshop on Parsing Technologies, pp. 85-94.

Grishman, R. (1995) *The NYU system for MUC-6 or where's the syntax?* In Proceedings of the 6th Message Understanding Conference (MUC-6), pp. 167-175.

Moon, T. K. (1996) *The Expectation-Maximization Algorithm*, IEEE Signal Processing Magazine, November, 1996, pp. 47-60.

Sproat R. and Chang N. (1994) *A Stochastic Finite-State Word-Segmentation Algorithm for Chinese.* In Proceeding of 32nd Annual Meeting of the Association for Computational Linguistics, pp. 66-73.

Yu, S., Bai S. and Wu P. (1998) *Description of the Kent Ridge Digital Labs System Used for MUC-7.* In Proceedings of the 7th Message Understanding Conference (MUC-7)

A Simple but Powerful Automatic Term Extraction Method

Hiroshi Nakagawa
Information Technology Center,
The University of Tokyo
7-3-1, Bunkyo, Hongo
Tokyo, Japan, 113-0033
nakagawa@r.dl.itc.u-tokyo.ac.jp

Tatsunori Mori
Yokohama National University
79-5, Tokiwadai,Hodogaya
Yokohama, Japan,240-0085
mori@forest.dnj.ynu.ac.jp

Abstract

In this paper, we propose a new idea for the automatic recognition of domain specific terms. Our idea is based on the statistics between a compound noun and its component single-nouns. More precisely, we focus basically on how many nouns adjoin the noun in question to form compound nouns. We propose several scoring methods based on this idea and experimentally evaluate them on the NTCIR1 TMREC test collection. The results are very promising especially in the low recall area.

Introduction

Automatic term recognition, ATR in short, aims at extracting domain specific terms from a corpus of a certain academic or technical domain. The majority of domain specific terms are compound nouns, in other words, uninterrupted collocations. 85% of domain specific terms are said to be compound nouns. They include single-nouns of the remaining 15% very frequently as their components, where "single-noun" means a noun which could not be further divided into several shorter and more basic nouns. In other words, the majority of compound nouns consist of the much smaller number of the remaining 15% single-noun terms and other single-nouns. In this situation, it is natural to pay attention to the relation among single-nouns and compound nouns, especially how single-noun terms contribute to make up compound noun terms.

Another important feature of domain specific terms is *termhood* proposed in (Kageura & Umino 96) where "termhood" refers to the degree that a linguistic unit is related to a domain-specific concept. Thus, what we really have to pursue is an ATR method which directly uses the notion of termhood.

Considering these factors, the way of making up compound nouns must be heavily related to the termhood of the compound nouns. The first reason is that termhood is usually calculated based on term frequency and bias of term frequency like inverse document frequency. Even though these calculations give a good approximation of termhood, still they are not directly related to termhood because these calculations are based on superficial statistics. That means that they are not necessarily meanings in a writer's mind but meanings in actual use. Apparently, termhood is intended to reflect this type of meaning. The second reason is that if a certain single-noun, say *N*, expresses the key concept of a domain that the document treats, the writer of the document must be using *N* not only frequently but also in various ways. For instance, he/she composes quite a few compound nouns using *N* and uses these compound nouns in documents he/she writes. Thus, we focus on the relation among single-nouns and compound nouns in pursuing new ATR methods.

The first attempt to make use of this relation has been done by (Nakagawa & Mori 98) through the number of distinct single-nouns that come to the left or right of a single-noun term when used in compound noun terms. Using this type of number associated with a single-noun term, Nakagawa and Mori proposed a scoring function for term candidates. Their term extraction method however is just one example of employing the relation among single-nouns and compound nouns. Note that this relation is essentially based on a noun bigram. In this paper, we expand the relation based on noun bigrams that might be the components of longer compound nouns. Then we experimentally evaluate the power of several variations of scoring functions based on the noun bigram relation using the NTCIR1 TMREC test collection. By this experimental clarification, we could conclude that the single-noun term's power of generating compound noun terms is useful and essential in ATR.

In this paper, section 1 gives the background of ATR methods. Section 2 describes the proposed method of the noun bigram based scoring function for term extraction. Section 3 describes the experimental results and discusses them.

1 Background

1.1 Candidates Extraction

The first thing to do in ATR is to extract *term candidates* from the given text corpus. Here we only focus on nouns, more precisely a single-noun and a compound noun, which are exactly the targets of the NTCIR1 TMREC task(Kageura et al 1999). To extract compound nouns which are promising term candidates and at the same time to exclude undesirable strings such as "*is a*" or "*of the*", the frequently used method is to filter out the words that are members of a *stop-word-list*. More complex structures like noun phrases, collocations and so on, become focused on (Frantzi and Ananiadou 1996). All of these are good term candidates in a corpus of a specific domain because all of them have a strong unithood (Kageura&Umino96) which refers to the degree of strength or stability of syntagmatic combinations or collocations. We assume the following about compound nouns or collocations:

Assumption *Terms having complex structure are to be made of existing simple terms*

The structure of complex terms is another important factor for automatic term candidates extraction. It is expressed syntactically or semantically. As a syntactic structure, dependency structures that are the results of parsing are focused on in many works. Since we focus on these complex structures, the first task in extracting term candidates is a morphological analysis including part of speech (POS) tagging. For Japanese, which is an agglutinative language, a morphological analysis was carried out which segmented words from a sentence and did POS tagging (Matsumoto et al. 1996).

After POS tagging, the complex structures mentioned above are extracted as term candidates. Previous studies have proposed many promising ways for this purpose, Hisamitsu(2000) and Nakagawa (1998) concentrated their efforts on compound nouns. Frantzi and Ananiadou (1996) tried to treat more general structures like collocations.

1.2 Scoring

The next thing to do is to assign a score to each term candidate in order to rank them in descending order of termhood. Many researchers have sought the definition of the term candidate's score which approximates termhood. In fact, many of those proposals make use of surface statistics like tf·idf. Ananiadou et al. proposed C-value (Frantzi and Ananiadou 1996) and NC-value (Frantzi and Ananiadou 1999) which count how independently the given compound noun is used in the given corpus. Hisamitsu (2000) propose a way to measure termhood that counts how far the given term is different from the distribution of non-domain-specific terms. All of them tried to capture how important and independent a writer regards and uses individual terms in a corpus

2 Single-Noun Bigrams as Components of Compound Nouns

2.1 Single-Noun Bigrams

The relation between a single-noun and complex nouns that include this single-noun is very important. Nevertheless, to our knowledge, this relation has not been paid enough attention so far. Nakagawa and Mori (1998) proposed a term scoring method that utilizes this type of relation. In this paper, we extend our idea comprehensively. Here we focus on compound nouns among the various types of complex terms. In technical documents, the majority of domain-specific terms are noun phrases or compound nouns consisting of a small number of single nouns. Considering this observation, we propose a new scoring method that measures the importance of each single-noun. In a nutshell, this scoring method for a single-noun measures how many distinct compound nouns contain a particular single-noun as their part in a given document or corpus. Here, think about the situtation where single-noun N occurs with other single-nouns which might be a part of many compound nouns shown in Figure 1 where [N M] means bigram of noun N and M.

[LN1 N] (#L1)	[N RN1](#R1)
:	:
[LNn N](LN)	[N RNm](#Rm)

Figure 1. Noun Bigram and their Frequency

In Figure 1, [LNi N] (i=1,..,n) and [N RNj] (j=1,...,m) are single-noun bigrams which constitute (parts of) compound nouns. #Li and #Rj (i=1,..,n and j=1,..,m) mean the frequency of the bigram [LNi N] and [N RNj] respectively. Note that since we depict only bigrams, compound nouns like [LNi N RNj] which contains [LNi N] and/or [N RNj] as their parts might actually occur in a corpus. Again this noun trigram might be a part of longer compound nouns.

Let us show an example of a noun bigram. Suppose that we extract compound nouns including "trigram" as candidate terms from a corpus shown in the following example.

Example 1.

trigram statistics, word trigram, class trigram, word trigram, trigram acquisition, word trigram statistics, character trigram

Then, noun bigrams consisting of a single-noun "trigram" are shown in the following where the number bewteen (and) shows the frequency.

word trigram (3) trigram statistics (2)
class trigram (1) trigram acquisition (1)
character trigram(1)

Figure 2. An example of noun bigram

We just focus on and utilize single-noun bigrams to define the function on which scoring is based. Note that we are concerned only with single-noun bigrams and not with a single-noun per se. The reason is that we try to sharply focus on the fact that the majority of domain specific terms are compound nouns. Compound nouns are well analyzed as noun bigram.

2.2 Scoring Function

2.2.1 The direct score of a noun bigram

Since a scoring function based on [LNi N] or [N RNj] could have an infinite number of variations, we here consider the following simple but representative scoring functions.

#LDN(N) and **#RDN(N)** : These are the number of distinct single-nouns which directly precede or succeed **N**. These are exactly "n" and "m" in Figure 1. For instance, in an example shown in Figure 2, #LDN(trigram)=3, #RDN(trigram)=2

LN(N,k) and **RN(N,k)**: The general functions that take into account the number of occurrences of each noun bigram like [LNi N] and [N RNj] are defined as follows.

$$\mathbf{LN(N,k)} = \sum_{i=1}^{\#LDN(N)} (\#\mathbf{Li})^{k} \quad (1)$$

$$\mathbf{RN(N,k)} = \sum_{j=1}^{\#RDN(N)} (\#\mathbf{Rj})^{k} \quad (2)$$

We can find various functions by varying parameter k of (1) and (2). For instance, #LDN(N) and #RDN(N) can be defined as **LN(N,0)** and **RN(N,0)**. **LN(N,1)** and **RN(N,1)** are the frequencies of nouns that directly precede or succeed **N**. In the example shown in Figure 2, for example, LN(trigram,1)=5, and RN(trigram,1)=3. Now we think about the nature of (1) and (2) with various value of the parameter k. The larger k is, the more we take into account the frequencies of each noun bigram. One extreme is the case k=0, namely LN(N,0) and RN(N,0), where we do not take into account the frequency of each noun bigram at all. LN(N,0) and RN(N,0) describe how linguistically and domain dependently productive the noun N is in a given corpus. That means that noun N presents a key and/or basic concept of the domain treated by the corpus. Other extreme cases are large k, like k=2 , 4, etc. In these cases, we rather focus on frequency of each noun bigram. In other words, statistically biased use of noun N is the main concern. In the example shown in Figure 2, for example, LN(trigram,2)=11, and RN(trigram,2)=5. If k<0, we discount the frequency of each noun bigram. However, this case does not show good results of in our ATR experiment.

2.2.2 Score of compound nouns

The next thing to do is to extend the scoring functions of a single-noun to the scoring functions of a compound noun. We adopt a very simple method, namely a geometric mean. Now think about a compound noun : CN = $N_1 N_2 \ldots N_L$. Then a geometric mean: **GM** of CN is defined as follows.

GM(CN,k)

$$= \left(\prod_{i=1}^{L} (LN(N_i,k)+1)(RN(N_i,k)+1) \right)^{\frac{1}{2L}} \quad -(3)$$

For instance, if we use LN(N,1) and RN(N,1) in example 1, GM(trigram,1) = $\sqrt{(3+1)\times(5+1)}$ = 4.90. In (3), GM does not depend on the length of a compound noun that is the number of single-nouns within the compound noun. This is because we have not yet had any idea about the relation between the importance of a compound noun and a length of the compound noun. It is fair to treat all compound nouns, including single-nouns, equally no matter how long or short each compound noun is.

2.2.3 Combining Compound Noun Frequency

Information we did not use in the bigram based methods described in 2.2.1 and 2.2.2 is the frequency of single-nouns and compound-nouns that occur independently, namely left and right adjacent words not being nouns. For instance, "word patterns" occurs independently in "... use the word patterns occurring in ... ." Since the scoring functions proposed in 2.2.1 are noun bigram statistics, the number of this kind of independent occurrences of nouns themselves are not used. If we take this information into account, a new type of information is used and better results are expected.

In this paper, we employ a very simple method for this. We observe that if a single-noun or a compound noun occurs independently, the score of the noun is multiplied by the number of its independent occurrences. Then GM(CN,k) of the formula (3) is revised. We call this new GM **FGM(CN,k)** and define it as follows.

if N occurs independently
then $\mathbf{FGM(CN,k)} = \mathbf{GM(CN,k)} \times \mathbf{f(CN)}$
where f(CN) means the number of independent occurrences of noun CN --- (4)

For instance, in example 1, if we find independent "trigram" three times in the corpus, FGM(trigram,1)= $3 \times \sqrt{(3+1)\times(5+1)}$ =14.70

2.2.4 Modified C-value

We compare our methods with the C-value based method(Frantzi and Ananiadou 1996) because 1) their method is very powerful to extract and properly score compound nouns., and 2) their method is basically based on unithood. On the contrary, our scoring functions proposed in 2.2.1 try to capture termhood. However the original definition of C-value can not score a single-noun because the important part of the definition C-value is:

$$\text{C-value}(a) = (\text{length}(a) - 1)(n(a) - \frac{t(a)}{c(a)}) \quad \text{--- (5)}$$

where a is compound noun, length(a) is the number of single-nouns which make up a, n(a) is the total frequency of occurrence of a on the corpus, t(a) is the frequency of occurrence of a in longer candidate terms, and c(a) is the number of those candidate terms.

As known from (5), all single-noun's C-value come to be 0. The reason why the first term of right hand side is (length(a)-1) is that C-value originally seemed to capture how much computational effort is to be made in order to recognize the important part of the term. Thus, if the length(a) is 1, we do not need any effort to recognize its part because the term a is a single-word and does not have its part. But we intend to capture how important the term is for the writer or reader, namely its termhood. In order to make the C-value capture termhood, we modify (5) as follows.

$$\text{MC-value}(a) = \text{length}(a)(n(a) - \frac{t(a)}{c(a)}) \quad (6)$$

Where "**MC-value**" means "Modified C-value."

3 Experimental Evaluation

3.1 Experiment

In our experiment, we use the NTCIR1 TMREC test collection (Kageura et al 1999). As an activity of TMREC, they have provided us with a Japanese test collection of a term recognition task. The goal of this task is to automatically recognize and extract terms from a text corpus which contains 1,870 abstracts gathered from the computer science and communication engineering domain corpora of the NACSIS Academic Conference Database, and 8,834 manually collected correct terms. The TMREC text corpus is morphologically analyzed and POS tagged by hand. From this POS tagged text, we extract uninterrupted noun sequences as term candidates. Actually 16,708 term candidates are extracted and several scoring methods are applied to them. All the extracted term candidates CNs are ranked according to their GM(CN,k), FGM(CN,k) and MC-value(CN) in descending order. As for parameter **k** of (1) and (2), we choose **k=1** because its performance is the best among various values of **k** in the range from 0 to 4. Thus, henceforth, we omit **k** from GM and FGM, like GM(CN) and FGM(CN). We use GM(CN) as the baseline.

In evaluation, we conduct experiments where we pick up the highest ranked term candidate down to the PNth highest ranked term candidate by these three scoring methods, and evaluate the set of selected terms with the number of correct terms, we call it CT, within it. In the following figures, we only show CT because recall is CT/8834, where 8834 is the number of all correct terms, precision is CT/PN.

Another measure NTCIR1 provides us with is the terms which include the correct term as its part. We call it "longer term" or LT. They are sometimes valued terms and also indicate in what context the correct terms are used. Then we also use the number of longer terms in our evaluation.

3.2 Results

In Figure 3 through 5, PN of X-axis means PN.

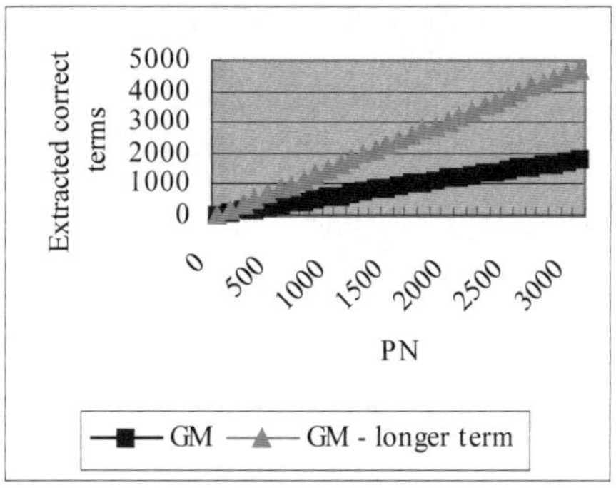

Figure 3. CT and LT of GM(CN) for each PN

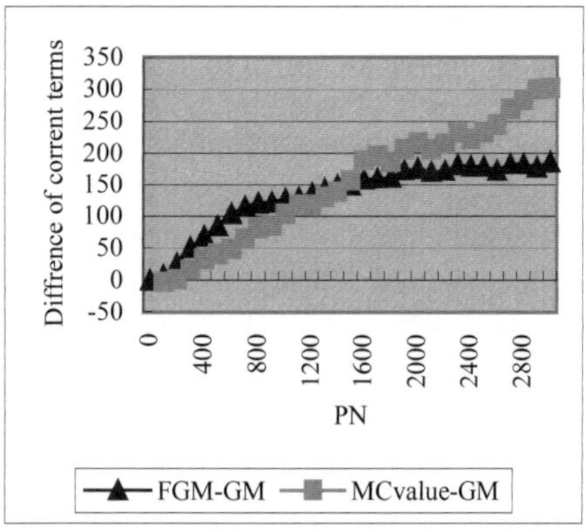

Figure 4. CT of FGM(CN) minus CT of GM(CN), and CT of MC-value(CN) minus CT of GM(CN) for each PN

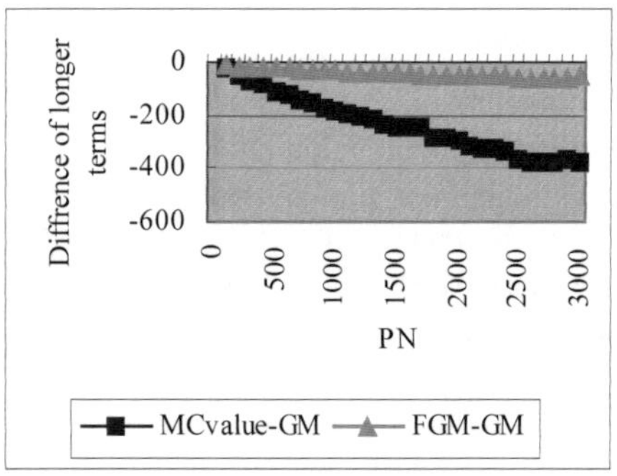

Figure 5. LT of GM(CN) minus LT of FGM(CN) , and LT of GM(CN) minus LT of MC-value(CN) for each PN

In Figure 3, the Y-axis represents CT in other words the number of correct terms picked up by GM(CN) and the number of longer terms picked up by GM(CN) for each PN. They are our baseline. The Figure 4 shows the difference between CT of FGM(CN) and CT of GM(CN) and the difference between CT of MC-value(CN) and CT of GM(CN) for each PN. Figure 5 shows the difference between LT of GM(CN) and LT of FGM(CN) or LT of MC-value(CN) for each PN. As known from Figure 4, FGM based method outperforms MC-value up to 1,400 highest ranked terms. Since in the domains of TMREC task that are computer science and communication engineering, 1,400 technical terms are important core terms, FGM method we propose is very promising to extract and recognize domain specific terms. We also show CT of each method for larger PN, say, from 3000 up to 15000 in Table 1 and 2.

Table 1. CT of each ranking method for PN larger than 3000

PN	GM	FGM	MC-value
3000	1784	1970	2111
6000	3286	3456	3671
9000	4744	4866	4930
12000	6009	6090	6046
15000	7042	7081	7068

Table 2. LT of each ranking method for PN larger than 3000

PN	GM	FGM	MC-Value
3000	2893	2840	2531
6000	5644	5576	5011
9000	8218	8152	7578
12000	10523	10488	9852
15000	12174	12186	12070

As seen in these figures and tables, if we want more terms about these domains, MC-value is more powerful, but when PN is larger than 12,000, again FGM outperforms. As for recognizing longer terms, GM(CN), which is the baseline, performs best for every PN. MC-value is the worst. From this observation we come to know that MC-value tends to assign higher score to shorter terms than GM or FGM. We are also interested in what kind of term is favored by each method. For this, we show the average length of the highest PN ranked terms of each method in Figure 6 where length of CN means the number of single-words CN consists of. Clearly, GM prefers longer terms. So does FGM. On the contrary, MC-value prefers shorter terms. However, as shown in Figure 6, the average length of the MC-value is more fluctuating. That means GM and FGM have more consistent tendency in ranking compound nouns. Finally we compare our results with NTCIR1 results (Kageura et al 1999). Unfortunately since (Kageura et al 1999) only provides the number of the all extracted terms and also the number of the all extracted correct terms, we could not directly compare our results with other NTCIR1 participants. Then, what is important is the fact that we extracted 7,082 correct terms from top 15,000 term candidates with the FGM methods. This fact is indicating that our methods show the highest performance among all other participants of NTCIR1 TMREC task because 1) the highest number of terms within the top 16,000 term candidates is 6,536 among all the participants of NTCIR1 TMREC task, and 2) the highest number or terms in all the participants of NTCIR1 TMREC task is 7,944, but they are extracted from top 23,270 term candidates, which means extremely low precision.

Conclusion

In this paper, we introduce a new ngle-noun bigram based statistical methods for ATR, which capture how many nouns adjoin the single-noun in question to form compound nouns. Through experimental evaluation using the NTCIR1 TMREC test collection, the FGM method we proposed showed the best performance in selecting up to 1,400 domain specific terms.

Acknowledgements

This research is funded by the Ministry of Education Science and Academic, Japan.

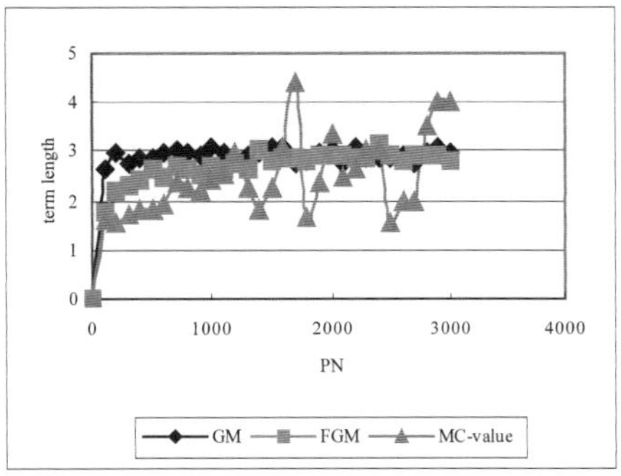

Figure 6. The average length of extracted terms by GM(CN), FGM(CN) and MC-value(CN) for each PN

References

Frantzi, T.K. and Ananiadou, S. 1996. "Extracting nested collocations". In *Proceedings of 16th International Conference on Computational Linguistics*, 41-46.

Frantzi, T.K. and Ananiadou, S. 1999. "The c-value/nc-value method for atr". *Journal of Natural Language Processing* 6(3), 145-179.

Hisamitsu, T, 2000. "A Method of Measuring Term Representativeness". In *Proceedings of 18th International Conference on Computational Linguistics*, 320-326.

Kageura, K. and Umino, B. 1996. "Methods of automatic term recognition: a review". *Terminology* 3(2), 259-289.

Kageura, K. et al, 1999. "TMREC Task: Overview and Evaluation". In *Proceedings of the First NTCIR Workshop on Research in Japanese Text Retrieval and Term Recognition*, 411-440.

Matsumoto, Y., Kurohashi, S., Yamaji, O., Taeki, H. and Nagao, M. 1996. *Instruction Manual of Japanese Morphological Analyzer JUMAN3.1.* Nagao Lab. at Kyoto University.

Nakagawa, H. and Mori, T. 1998. "Nested Collocation and Compound Noun for Term Recognition". In *Proceedings of the First Workshop on Computational Terminology COMPTERM'98*, 64-70.

Automatic Discovery of Term Similarities Using Pattern Mining

Goran NENADIĆ, Irena SPASIĆ and Sophia ANANIADOU

Computer Science, University of Salford
Salford, M5 4WT, UK
{G.Nenadic, I.Spasic, S.Ananiadou}@salford.ac.uk

Abstract

Term recognition and clustering are key topics in automatic knowledge acquisition and text mining. In this paper we present a novel approach to the automatic discovery of term similarities, which serves as a basis for both classification and clustering of domain-specific concepts represented by terms. The method is based on automatic extraction of significant patterns in which terms tend to appear. The approach is domain independent: it needs no manual description of domain-specific features and it is based on knowledge-poor processing of specific term features. However, automatically collected patterns are domain specific and identify significant contexts in which terms are used. Beside features that represent contextual patterns, we use lexical and functional similarities between terms to define a combined similarity measure. The approach has been tested and evaluated in the domain of molecular biology, and preliminary results are presented.

Introduction

In a knowledge intensive discipline such as molecular biology, the vast and constantly increasing amount of information demands innovative techniques to gather and systematically structure knowledge, usually available only from text/document resources. In order to discover new knowledge, one has to identify main concepts, which are linguistically represented by domain specific terms (Maynard and Ananiadou (2000)). There is an increased amount of new terms that represent newly created concepts. Since existing term dictionaries usually do not meet the needs of specialists, automatic term extraction tools are indispensable for efficient term discovery and dynamic update of term dictionaries.

However, automatic term recognition (ATR) is not the ultimate aim: terms recognised should be related to existing knowledge and/or to each other. This entails the fact that terms should be classified or clustered so that semantically similar terms are grouped together. Classification and/or clustering of terms are indispensable for improving information extraction, knowledge acquisition, and document categorisation. Classification can also be used for efficient term management and populating and updating existing ontologies in a consistent manner. Both classification and clustering methods are built on top of a specific similarity measure. The notion of term similarity has been defined and considered in different ways: terms can have functional and/or structural similarities, though they can be correlated by different relationships (Grefenstette (1994), Maynard and Ananiadou (2000)). In this paper we suggest a novel, domain-independent method for the automatic discovery of term similarities, which can serve as a basis for both classification and clustering of terms. The method is mainly based on the automatic discovery of significant term features through pattern mining. Automatically collected patterns are domain dependent and they identify significant contexts in which terms tend to appear. In addition, the measure combines lexical and syntactical similarities between terms.

The paper is organised as follows. In Section 1 we overview term management approaches. Section 2 introduces the term similarity measure and Section 3 presents results and experiments.

1 Terminology Management

Since vast amount of knowledge still remains unexplored, several systems have been proposed to help scientists to acquire relevant knowledge from scientific literature. For example, GENIES (Friedman et al. (2001)) uses a semantic grammar and substantial syntactic knowledge in order to extract comprehensive information about signal-transduction pathways. Some of the systems are terminology-based, since technical terms semantically characterise documents and therefore represent starting place for knowledge acquisition tasks. For example, Mima et al. (2002) introduce TIMS, a terminology-based knowledge acquisition system, which integrates automatic term recognition, term variation management, context-based automatic term clustering, ontology-based inference, and intelligent tag information retrieval. The system's aim is to provide efficient access and integration of heterogeneous biological textual data and databases.

There are numerous approaches to ATR. Some methods (Bourigault (1992), Ananiadou (1994)) rely purely on linguistic information, namely morpho-syntactic features of term candidates. Recently, hybrid approaches combining linguistic and statistical knowledge are becoming increasingly used (Frantzi et al. (2000), Nakagawa et al. (1998)).

There is a range of clustering and classification approaches that are based on statistical measures of word co-occurrences (e.g. Ushioda (1996)), or syntactic information derived from corpora (e.g. Grefenstette (1994)). However, few of them deal with term clustering: Maynard and Ananiadou (2000) present a method that uses manually defined semantic frames for specific classes, Hatzivassiloglou et al. (2001) use machine learning techniques to disambiguate names of proteins, genes and RNAs, while Friedman et al. (2001) describe extraction of specific molecular pathways from journal articles.

In our previous work, an integrated knowledge mining system in the domain of molecular biology, ATRACT, has been developed (Mima et al. (2001)). ATRACT (**A**utomatic **T**erm **R**ecognition and **C**lustering for **T**erms) is a part of the ongoing BioPath[1] project, and its main aim is to facilitate an efficient expert-computer interaction during term-based knowledge acquisition. Term management is based on integration of automatic term recognition and automatic term clustering (ATC). ATR is based on the *C/NC-value* method (Frantzi et al. (2000)), a hybrid approach combining *linguistic knowledge* (term formation patterns) and *statistical knowledge* (term length, frequency of occurrence, etc). The extension of the method handles orthographic, morphological and syntactic term variants and acronym recognition as an integral part of the ATR process (Nenadić et al. (2002a)), providing that all term occurrences of a term are considered. The ATC method is based on the Ushioda's AMI (Average Mutual Information) hierarchical clustering method (Ushioda (1996)). Co-occurrence based term similarities are used as input, and a dendrogram of terms is generated.[2]

2 Term Similarity Measures

In this section we introduce a novel hybrid method to measure term similarity. Our method incorporates three types of similarity measures, namely contextual, lexical and syntactical similarity. We use a linear combination of the three similarities in order to estimate similarity between terms. In the following subsections we describe each of the three similarity measures.

2.1 Contextual Similarity

Determining the similarity of terms based on their contexts is a standard approach based on the hypothesis that similar terms tend to appear in similar contexts. Contextual similarity, however, may be determined in a number of ways depending on the way in which the context is defined. For example, some approaches consider only terms that appear in a close proximity to each other (Maynard and Ananiadou (2000)), while in other approaches, grammatical roles such as object or subject are taken into account (Grefenstette (1994)).

Our approach to contextual similarity is based on automatic *pattern mining*. The aim is to automatically identify and learn the most important context patterns in which terms appear. *Context pattern* (CP) is a generalised regular expression that corresponds to either left or right context of a term.[3] The following example shows a sample left context pattern of the term `high affinity`:

[1] BioPath is a Eureka funded project, coordinated by LION BioScience (http://www.lionbioscience.com) and funded by the German Ministry of Research.

[2] For the evaluation of the ATR and ATC methods incorporated in ATRACT, see Mima et al. (2001).

[3] Left and right contexts are treated separately.

`V:bind TERM:rxr_heterodimers PREP:with`

Let us now describe the process of constructing CPs and determining their importance. First, we collect concordances for all automatically recognised terms. Context constituents, which we consider important for discriminating terms (e.g. noun and verb phrases, prepositions, and terms themselves) are identified by a tagger and by appropriate local grammars, which define syntactic phrases (e.g. NPs, VPs). The grammatical and lexical information attached to the context constituents is used to construct CPs. In the simplest case, contexts are mapped into the syntactic categories of their constituents. However, the lemmatised form for each of the syntactic categories can be used as well. For example, when encountered in a context, the preposition `with` can be either mapped to its POS tag, i.e. `PREP`, or instead, the lemma can be added, in which case we have an *instantiated* chunk: `PREP:with`. Further, some of the syntactic categories can be removed from the context patterns, as not all syntactic categories are equally significant in providing useful contextual information (Maynard and Ananiadou (2000)). Such CPs will be regarded as *normalised* CPs. In our approach, one can define which categories to instantiate and which to remove. In the examples provided later in the paper (Section 3) we decided to remove the following categories: adjectives (that are not part of a term), adverbs, determiners and so-called linking words (e.g. `however`, `moreover`, etc.). Also, we instantiated terms and either verbs or prepositions, as these categories are significant for discriminating terms.

Once we have normalised CPs, we calculate the values of a measure called *CP-value* in order to estimate the importance of the CPs. CP-value is defined similarly to the C/NC-value for terms (Frantzi et al. (2000)). It assesses a CP (p) according to its total frequency ($f(p)$), its length ($|p|$, as the number of constituents) and the frequency of its occurrence within other CPs ($|T_p|$, where T_p is a set of all CPs that contain p):

$$CP(p)=\begin{cases}\log_2|p|\cdot f(p); & p \text{ is not nested}\\ \log_2|p|\cdot\left(f(p)-\dfrac{1}{|T_p|}\sum_{b\in Tp} f(b)\right) & \text{; otherwise}\end{cases}$$

The CPs whose CP-value is above a chosen threshold are deemed important. Note that these patterns are domain-specific and that they are automatically extracted from a domain specific corpus. Tables 1 and 2 show samples of significant left context patterns extracted from a MEDLINE corpus (MEDLINE (2002)).

CPs	CP-value
PREP NP	272.65
PREP NP PREP	186.47
. . .	. . .
PREP NP V:*stimulate*	9.32
V:*indicate* NP	5.00
PREP NP PREP V:*involve* NP	4.64
PREP TERM:*transcriptional_activity*	4.47
V:*require* NP PREP	4.38
PREP TERM:*nuclear_receptor* PREP	4.00

Table 1: Sample of left CPs
(only terms and most frequent verbs are instantiated)

CPs	CP-value
PREP:*of* NP	121.49
V NP	71.42
PREP:*of* NP V	62.83
NP PREP:*of* NP	59.72
PREP:*in* NP	59.55
NP PREP:*of*	43.37
PREP:*of* NP V NP	37.64
PREP:*of* TERM:*transcriptional_activity*	36.60

Table 2: Sample of left CPs
(only terms and prepositions are instantiated)

At this point, each term is associated with a set of the most characteristic patterns in which it occurs. We treat CPs as term features, and we use a feature contrast model (Santini and Jain (1999)) to calculate similarity between terms as a function of both common and distinctive features. Let us now formally define the contextual similarity measure. Let C_1 and C_2 be two sets of CPs associated with terms t_1 and t_2 respectively. Then, the *contextual similarity* (*CS*) between t_1 and t_2 corresponds to the ratio between the number of common and distinctive contexts:

$$CS(t_1,t_2)=\frac{2|C_1\cap C_2|}{2|C_1\cap C_2|+|C_1\setminus C_2|+|C_1\setminus C_2|}$$

2.2 Lexical Similarity

We also examine the lexical similarity between words that constitute terms. For example, if terms share the same head, they are assumed to have the same concept as an (in)direct hypernym (e.g. `progesterone receptor` and `oestrogen receptor`). Further, if one of such terms has additional modifiers, this may indicate concept specialisation (e.g. `nuclear receptor` and `orphan nuclear receptor`). Bearing that in mind, we base the definition of lexical similarity on having a common head and/or modifier(s). Formally, if t_1 and t_2 are terms, H_1 and H_2 their heads, and M_1 and M_2 the sets of the stems of their modifiers, then their *lexical similarity* (*LS*) is calculated according to the following formula:

$$LS(t_1,t_2) = \frac{1}{a+b}\left(a * |H_1 \cap H_2| + b * \frac{2|M_1 \cap M_2|}{2|M_1 \cap M_2| + |M_1 \setminus M_2| + |M_1 \setminus M_2|}\right)$$

where a and b are weights such that $a > b$, since we give higher priority to shared heads over shared modifiers.

Note that the lexical similarity between two different terms can have a positive value only if at least one of them is a multiword term. Also, when calculating lexical similarity between terms that are represented by corresponding acronyms, we use normalised expanded forms.[4]

2.3 Syntactical Similarity

By analysing the distribution of similar terms in corpora, we observed that some general (i.e. domain independent) lexico-syntactic patterns indicate functional similarity between terms. For instance, the following example:

... steroid receptors *such as* estrogen receptor, glucocorticoid receptor, *and* progesterone receptor.

suggests that all the terms involved are highly correlated, since they appear in an enumeration (represented by the *such-as* pattern) which indicates their similarity (based on the *is_a* relationship). Some of these patterns have been previously used to discover hyponym relations between words (Hearst (1992)). We generalised the approach by taking into account patterns in which the terms are used *concurrently* within the same context. We hypothesise that the parallel usage of terms within the same context, as a specific type of co-occurrence, shows their functional similarity. Namely, all the terms within a parallel structure have the same *syntactic* function within the sentence (e.g. object or subject) and are used in combination with the same verb or preposition. This fact is used as an indicator of their semantic similarity.

In our approach, several types of lexico-syntactical patterns are considered: enumeration expressions, coordination, apposition, and anaphora. However, currently we do not discriminate between different similarity relationships among terms (which are represented by different patterns), but instead, we consider terms appearing in the same syntactical roles as highly semantically correlated.

A sample of enumeration patterns is shown in Table 3.[5] Manually defined patterns are applied as syntactic filters in order to retrieve sets of similar terms. These patterns provide relatively good recall and precision. We also used coordination patterns (Klavans et al. (1997)) as another type of parallel syntactic structure. Two types of argument coordination and two types of head coordination patterns were considered (see Table 4). However, not all the sequences that match the coordination patterns are coordinated structures (see Table 5). Therefore, these patterns provide relatively good recall, but not high precision if one wants to retrieve terms involved in such expression.[6] However, both term coordination and (nominal) conjunction of terms indicate their similarity.

Based on co-occurrence of terms in these parallel lexico-syntactical patterns, we define the *syntactical similarity* (*SS*) measure for a pair of terms as 1 if the two terms appear together in any of the patterns, and 0 otherwise.

---

[4] For our approach to acronym acquisition and term normalisation, see Nenadic et al. (2002).

[5] Non-terminal syntactic categories are given in angle brackets. Non-terminal <**&**> denotes a conjunctive word sequence, i.e. the following regular expression: **(as well as)** | **(and[/or])** | **(or[/and])**. Special characters (,), [,], |, and * have the usual interpretation in regular expression notation.

[6] In the experiments that we have performed, the precision of expanding terms from coordinated structures was 70%.

<table>
<tr><td><TERM>([(](such as)|like|(e.g.[,])) <TERM> (,<TERM>)* [[,] <&> <TERM>] [)]</td></tr>
<tr><td><TERM> (,<TERM>)* [,] <&> other <TERM></td></tr>
<tr><td><TERM> [,] (including|especially) <TERM> (,<TERM>)* [[,] <&> <TERM>]</td></tr>
<tr><td>both <TERM> and <TERM></td></tr>
<tr><td>either <TERM> or <TERM></td></tr>
<tr><td>neither <TERM> nor <TERM></td></tr>
</table>

Table 3: Sample of enumeration lexico-syntactic patterns

<table>
<tr><td>(<N>|<Adj>) (,(<N>|<Adj>))* [,] <&> (<N>|<Adj>) <TERM></td></tr>
<tr><td>(<N>|<Adj>)/(<N>|<Adj>) <TERM></td></tr>
<tr><td>(<N>|<Adj>) <TERM> (,<TERM>)* [,] <&> <TERM></td></tr>
<tr><td>(<N>|<Adj>) <TERM>/<TERM></td></tr>
</table>

Table 4: Sample of coordination patterns

head coordination	[adrenal [glands and gonads]]
term conjunction	[adrenal glands] and [gonads]

Table 5: Ambiguities of coordinated structures

2.4 Hybrid CLS Similarity

None of the similarities introduced so far is sufficient on its own to reliably estimate similarity between two arbitrary terms. For example, if a term appears infrequently or within very specific CPs, the number of its significant CPs will influence its contextual similarity to other terms. Further, there are concepts that have idiosyncratic names (e.g. a protein named `Bride of sevenless`), which thus cannot be classified relying exclusively on lexical similarity. Our experiments also show that syntactical similarity provides high precision, but low recall when used on its own, as not all terms appear in a parallel lexico-syntactical expression.

Therefore, we introduce a hybrid term similarity measure, called the *CLS* similarity, as a linear combination of the three similarity measures:

$$CLS(t_1, t_2) = \alpha\, CS(t_1, t_2) + \beta\, LS(t_1, t_2) + \gamma\, SS(t_1, t_2)$$

The choice of the weights α, β, and γ in the previous formula is not a trivial problem. In our preliminary experiments (Section 3) we used manually chosen values. However, the parameters have also been fine-tuned automatically by supervised learning method based on a genetic algorithm approach (Spasić et al. (2002)). A domain specific ontology has been used to evaluate the generated similarity measures and to set the direction of their convergence. The differences between results based on the various parameters are presented in the following section.

3 Results, Evaluation and Discussion

The *CLS* measure was tested on a corpus of 2008 abstracts retrieved from MEDLINE database (MEDLINE (2002)) with manually chosen values 0.3, 0.3 and 0.4 for α, β, and γ respectively. Random samples of results have been evaluated by a domain expert, and the combined measure proved to be a good indicator of semantic similarity. Table 6 shows the similarity of term `retinoic acid receptor` to a number of terms. The examples point out the importance of combining different types of term similarities. For instance, the low value of contextual similarity[7] for `retinoid X receptor` is balanced out by the other two similarity values, thus correctly indicating it as a term similar to term `retinoic acid receptor`. Similarly, the high value of the contextual similarity for `signal transduction pathway` is neutralised by the other two similarity

[7] The low value is caused by relatively low frequency of the term's occurrences in the corpus.

values, hence preventing it as being labelled as similar to `retinoic acid receptor`.

Term	*CS*	*SS*	*LS*	*CLS*
nuclear receptor	0.58	1.00	0.50	0.72
retinoid X receptor	0.32	1.00	0.33	0.60
retinoic acid	0.31	0.00	1.00	0.39
receptor complex	0.52	0.00	0.50	0.31
progesteron receptor	0.35	0.00	0.50	0.25
signal transduction pathway	0.75	0.00	0.00	0.22

Table 6: Similarity values between `retinoic acid receptor` and other terms

The combined measure also proved to be consistent in the sense that similar terms share the same "friends" (Maynard and Ananiadou (2000)). For example, the similarity values of two similar terms `glucocorticoid receptor` and `estrogen receptor` (the value of their similarity is 0.68) with respect to other terms are mainly approximate (Table 7).

Term	glucocotricoid receptor	estrogen receptor
steroid receptor	0.66	0.64
progesterone receptor	0.55	0.59
human estrogen	0.28	0.37
retinoid x receptor	0.27	0.36
nuclear receptor	0.30	0.33
receptor complex	0.31	0.33
retinoic acid receptor	0.27	0.28
retinoid nuclear	0.26	0.26

Table 7: Similarity values for `glucocorticoid receptor` and `estrogen receptor`

The supervised learning of parameters resulted in the values 0.13, 0.81 and 0.06 for α, β, and γ respectively (see Spasić et al. (2002)). The measure with these values showed a higher degree of stability relative to the ontology-based similarity measure. Note that the lexical similarity appears to be the most important and the syntactical similarity to be insignificant. The ontology used as a seed for learning term similarities contained well-structured, standardised and preferred terms which resulted in promoting the lexical similarity as the most significant. On the other hand, the *SS* similarity is corpus-dependent: the size of the corpus and the frequency with which the concurrent lexico-syntactic patterns are realised in it, affect the syntactical similarity. In the training corpus such patterns occurred infrequently relative to the number of terms, which indicates that a bigger corpus is needed in the training phase. In order to increase the number of concurrent patterns, we also aim at including additional patterns that describe appositions and implementing procedures for resolution of co-referring terms. We also plan to experiment with parametrising the values of syntactical similarity depending on the number and type of patterns in which two terms appear simultaneously.

The main purpose of discovering term similarities is to produce a similarity matrix to identify term clusters. In Nenadić et al. (2002b) we present some preliminary results on term clustering using the *CLS* hybrid term similarity measure. Two different methods (namely the nearest neighbour and the Ward's method) have been used, and both achieved around 70% precision in clustering semantically similar terms.

Conclusions and Further Research

In this paper we have presented a novel method for the automatic discovery of term similarities. The method is based on the combination of contextual, lexical and syntactical similarities between terms. Lexical similarity exposes the resemblance between the words that constitute terms, while syntactical similarity is based on mutual co-occurrence in parallel lexico-syntactic patterns. Contextual similarity is based on the automatic discovery of significant contexts through contextual pattern mining. Although the approach is domain independent and knowledge-poor, automatically collected patterns are domain specific and they identify significant contexts in which terms tend to appear. However, in order to learn domain-appropriate term similarity parameters, we need to customise the method by incorporating domain-specific knowledge. For example, we have used an ontology to represent such knowledge.

The preliminary results in the domain of molecular biology have shown that the measure proves to be a good indicator of semantic similarity between terms. Furthermore, the similarity measure is consistent at assigning weights: similar terms tend to share the same "friends", i.e. there is a significant degree of overlapping between terms that are similar. These results are encouraging, as terms are grouped reliably according to their contextual, syntactical and lexical similarities.

Besides term clustering (presented in Nenadić et al. (2002b)), the similarity measure can be used for several term-oriented knowledge management tasks. Our future work will focus on the term classification and the consistent population and update of ontologies. However, specific term relationship identification that will direct placing terms in a hierarchy is needed. Further, term similarities can be used for term sense disambiguation as well, which is essential for resolving terminological confusion occurring in many domains.

Acknowledgement

We would like to thank Dr. Sylvie Albert and Dr. Dietrich Schuhmann from LION Bioscience for the evaluation of the results.

References

Ananiadou S. (1994): *A Methodology for Automatic Term Recognition.* Proceedings of COLING-94, Kyoto, Japan.

Bourigault D. (1992): *Surface Grammatical Analysis for the Extraction of Terminological Noun Phrases.* Proceedings of 14th International Conference on Computational Linguistics, Nantes, France, pp. 977-981.

Frantzi K.T., Ananiadou S. and Mima H. (2000): *Automatic Recognition of Multi-Word Terms: the C-value/NC-value method.* International Journal on Digital Libraries, 3/2, pp. 115-130.

Friedman C., Kra P., Yu H., Krauthammer M. and Rzhetsky A. (2001): *GENIES: A Natural Language Processing System for the Extraction of Molecular Pathways from Journal Articles.* Bioinformatics, 17/1, pp. S74-S82.

Grefenstette G. (1994): *Exploration in Automatic Thesaurus Discovery.* Kluwer Academic Publishers, Massachusetts, p. 302.

Hatzivassiloglou V., Duboue P. and Rzetsky A. (2001): *Disambiguating Proteins, Genes, and RNA in Text: A Machine Learning Approach.* Bioinformatics, 17/1, pp. S97-S106

Hearst M.A. (1992): *Automatic acquisition of hyponyms from large text corpora.* Proceedings of the 14th International Conference on Computational Linguistics, Nantes, France.

Klavans J. L., Tzoukermann E. and Jacquemin C. (1997): *A Natural Language Approach to Multi-Word Term Conflation.* Proceedings of Workshop DELOS, Zurich, pp. 33-40.

Maynard D. and Ananiadou S. (2000): *Identifying Terms by Their Family and Friends.* Proceedings of COLING 2000, Luxembourg, pp.530-536.

MEDLINE (2002): *National Library of Medicine.* http://www.ncbi.nlm.nih.gov/PubMed/

Mima H., Ananiadou S. and Nenadić G. (2001): ATRACT Workbench: *An Automatic Term Recognition and Clustering of Terms.* Text, Speech and Dialogue - TSD 2001, LNAI 2166, Springer-Verlag, Berlin, pp. 126-133.

Mima H., Ananiadou S., Nenadić G. and Tsujii J. (2002): *A Methodology for Terminology-based Knowledge Acquisition and Integration.* Proceedings of COLING 2002, Taiwan

Nakagawa H. and Mori, T. (2000): *Nested Collocation and Compound Noun for Term Recognition.* Proceedings of the First Workshop on Computational Terminology COMPUTERM 98, pp. 64-70.

Nenadić G., Spasić I. and Ananiadou S. (2002a): *Automatic Acronym Acquisition and Term Variation Management within Domain-specific Texts.* Proceedings of LREC 2002, Las Palmas, Spain, pp. 2155-2162.

Nenadić G., Spasić I. and Ananiadou S. (2002b): *Term Clustering using a Corpus-Based Similarity Measure.* Text, Speech and Dialogue - TSD 2002, LNAI series, Springer-Verlag, Berlin

Santini S. and Jain R. (1999): *Similarity Measures.* IEEE Transactions on Pattern Analysis and Machine Intelligence, 21/9, pp. 871-88

Spasić I., Nenadić G. and Ananiadou S. (2002): *Supervised Learning of Term Similarities.* IDEAL 2002, LNAI series, Springer-Verlag, Berlin

Ushioda A. (1996): *Hierarchical Clustering of Words.* Proceedings of COLING '96, Copenhagen, pp. 1159-1162.

An LCS-Based Approach for Analyzing Japanese Compound Nouns with Deverbal Heads

Koichi Takeuchi, Kyo Kageura and Teruo Koyama
National Institute of Informatics
2-1-2 Hitotsubashi, Chiyoda-ku, Tokyo, 101-8430, Japan
{koichi,kyo,t_koyama}@nii.ac.jp

Abstract

This paper describes a principled approach for analyzing relations between constituent words of compound nouns whose heads are deverbal nouns. To develop an analyzer for the compound nouns with deverbal heads is an essential element of developing of a general compound analyzer, as they constitute a major part of the compound nouns. Our approach is based on the classification of deverbal nouns by their lexical conceptual structure (LCS) and the classification of nouns in general (to appear in the modifier position) vis-à-vis a few core LCS types (of head deverbal nouns). The experimental evaluation based on compound nouns with deverbal heads showed that over 99% of the compounds were accurately analyzed. The result of the experiment indicates that our approach is very promising.

1 Introduction

This paper proposes a principled approach to analyzing Japanese compound nouns whose heads are deverbal nouns (henceforth deverbal compounds for succinctness), using the framework of lexical conceptual structure (LCS).

Deverbal compounds constitute a major part of Japanese compound nouns, especially in technical terms where noun compounds are abundant[1] and to develop a method to deal with deverbal compounds is an essential element of developing a full-scale, high-performance compound noun analyzer. We focus on compounds with only two constituent words, as more complex compounds are basically constructed by the iteration of binary rules (Kageyama, 1999).

Deverbal nouns may behave as verbs, assigning thematic roles to the other noun constituent in a compound, or they may behave as nouns accepting a thematic role or modifying the other constituent. On this account, the relation between constituent words in a deverbal compound may be modification or *adjunct* relation (when the deverbal head functions as an ordinary noun), or it may be thematic role or *internal argument* relation (when the deverbal head takes a verbal role). Though there are various kinds of semantic relations that should be identified in compound nouns, the disambiguation of modification and internal argument is the first and essential element in compound noun analysis.

For the analysis of deverbal compounds, we propose a method based on LCS (Jackendoff, 1990; Kageyama, 1996). We will show that, by adopting LCS-based approach, it is possible to disambiguate the relation between constituent words in deverbal compounds with high accuracy. As LCS gives a clear framework for describing verb semantics, the lexicon of deverbal nouns can be constructed consistently and is thus extendable to a large scale, which is another advantage of the LCS-based method.

In the following, after briefly discussing the background and the overall framework of the approach, we sketch the basic idea of using LCS for the analysis of deverbal compounds. We will then elaborate our LCS system (TLCS) in section 4, noun classification in section 5, and procedure of analysis in section 6. In section 7, we will show the result of experimental evaluation, which is highly promising.

[1] For instance, the ratio of technical terms that contains deverbal nouns is 78% in a dictionary of information processing (Aiso, 1993)

2 Background

2.1 Previous work

The existing work on compound noun analyses takes either the statistical approach or the semantic approach. The former is more concerned with contextual aspects of compounding, while the latter with lexical aspects.

Lauer (1995) and Kobayasi et al. (1994) used corpus-based statistical techniques for bracketing compound nouns. Barker and Szpakowicz (1998) proposed a semi-automatic approach to analyzing and relations between constituents in nouns phrases. Statistical techniques are useful for broad-coverage shallow analysis when training methods are available.

On the other hand, semantic approaches explore types of relations between constituents in compounds (Levi, 1978; Isabelle, 1984). Iida et al. (1984) applied semantic framework of (Levi, 1978) and (Isabelle, 1984) to the analysis of English compounds. Semantic approaches are important for the deeper analysis, but the construction of the necessary lexicon tends to be too much dependent on a particular system and the lexicon is not easily extendable.

2.2 The basic design of our compound analyzer

In this paper we try to establish a semantic framework of the analysis of compound nouns without depending on particular applications or specific domain knowledge. It is because the formation of compound nouns mainly depends on lexical nature of their constituent words.

In semantic approach, it is important to clarify what kind of lexical nature is relevant to what kind of phenomena (i.e. relations) in what type of compound nouns, and to develop a framework and method of defining and describing the necessary semantic information consistently. The semantic framework should be clear enough so that the required lexicon can be extendable consistently to a very large size. The work reported in this paper, i.e. an LCS-based approach for deverbal compound analysis, constitutes a core of this overall framework.

3 Basic Framework: Compound Noun Analysis and TLCS

Recent studies in linguistics (Hale and Keyser, 1990; Rappaport and Levin, 1988; Jackendoff, 1990; Levin and Hovav, 1995; Kageyama, 1996; Sugioka, 1997; Sugioka, 2000) have shown that the semantic decomposition based on the LCS framework can systematically explain the word formation as well as the syntax structure. However existing LCS frameworks can not be applied to the analysis of compounds straightforwardly because they do not give restriction rules nor extensive semantic predicates for LCS. Therefore we construct an original LCS, called TLCS[2], based on the LCS framework with a clear set of LCS types and basic predicates. We use the acronym "TLCS" to avoid the confusion with other LCS-based schemes or with the general idea of LCS.

In this section we will briefly sketch how the expanded categories for nouns and deverbal nouns based on the TLCS framework can be used in disambiguating the intra-compound relations in deverbal compounds. Our framework, as having a formal structure and procedural restrictions, also has an advantage that the consistency of describing lexical meanings can be maintained.

3.1 Argument structure

The approach, using TLCS, is based on argument structure (Grimshaw, 1990). Argument structure is a simple semantic structure for a verb to express thematic role delivered to nouns which are arguments. There are two types arguments, i.e. external argument ('Agent') and internal argument ('Theme' and 'Goal')[3] For example, we describe the argument structure of a Japanese deverbal 'sousa' (operate) as follows:

sousa (operate): (Agent $\langle$ Theme $\rangle$).

Agent is the operator and Theme is the object that is operated. $\langle\cdot\rangle$ denotes an internal argument.

In deverbal compounds, it is only the internal arguments that can take a predicate-argument relation (Kageyama (1996)); elements of external arguments cannot establish a predicate-argument relation in deverbal compounds. This restriction is essential in disambiguating relations between constituent words in deverbal compounds.

[2] 'T' denotes the initial of terminology as well as the first author.

[3] In this paper, we limit the types of thematic role to three, i.e. Agent, Theme and Goal.

3.2 Relation between a noun and a deverbal noun

As mentioned, the relations between the words in Japanese deverbal compounds can be divided into two: (i) the modifier becomes an internal argument of the deverbal head, and (ii) the modifier functions as an adjunct. The disambiguation of these two relations is an essential element in compound noun analysis.[4]

Take, for example, the following two compounds[5]

kikai	-sousa	kikai	-hon'yaku
machine	-operate	machine	-translate
(machine operation)		(machine translation)	

The modifier 'kikai' is the internal argument of the deverbal head in the former, while it is the adjunct in the latter.

3.3 Compound noun analysis using TLCS

We assume that the relation can be determined by the combination of the TLCS on the side of deverbal heads and the consistent categorization of modifier nouns on the basis of their behavior vis-á-vis a few canonical TLCS types (or semantic predicates) of the deverbal heads. Figure 1 shows examples of disambiguating relations using the TLCS types of deverbal heads.

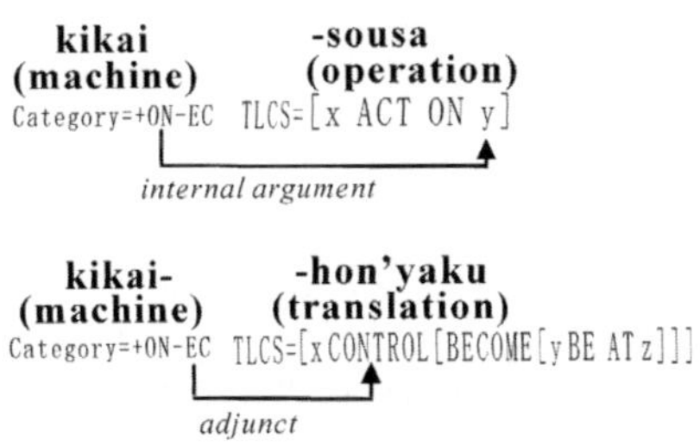

Figure 1: Disambiguating relations using TLCS types of deverbal heads.

The description in square brackets denotes the TLCS for the deverbal heads 'sousa' (operate) and 'hon'yaku' (translate). In TLCSes, the words written in capital letters are semantic predicates, 'x' denotes the external argument, and 'y' and 'z' denote the internal arguments. We will elaborate how the disambiguation is done in the following three sections.

4 TLCS

The first lexical information essential for the compound analyzer is the LCS-based classification scheme of deverbal nouns and the lexicon. Based on the existing work on LCS (Kageyama, 1996; Sugioka, 1997), we have established a TLCS, i.e. a set of original predicates and basic structure types that can describe the semantic structure of deverbal nouns for the Japanese compound noun analyzer.

Table 1: List of TLCS types

1 [x ACT ON y]
enzan (calculate), sousa (operate)
2 [x CONTROL[BECOME [y BE AT z]]]
kioku (memorize), hon'yaku (translate)
3 [x CONTROL[BECOME [y NOT BE AT z]]]
shahei (shield), yokushi (deter)
4 [x CONTROL [y MOVE TO z]]
densou (transmit), dempan (propagate)
5 [x=y CONTROL[BECOME [y BE AT z]]]
kaifuku (recover), shuuryou (close)
6 [BECOME[y BE AT z]]
houwa (become saturated)
bumpu (be distributed)
7 [y MOVE TO z]
idou (move), sen'i (transmit)
8 [x CONTROL[y BE AT z]]
iji (maintain), hogo (protect)
9 [x CONTROL[BECOME[x BE WITH y]]]
ninshiki (recognize), yosoku (predict)
10 [y BE AT z]
sonzai (exist), ichi (locate)
11 [x ACT]
kaigi (hold a meeting), gyouretsu (queue)
12 [x CONTROL[BECOME [[FILLED]y BE AT z]]]
shomei (sign-name)

We established 12 TLCSes as listed in Table 1.[6] The number attached to each TLCS type in Table 1 will be used throughout the paper

[4] The level of the analysis is language independent, and the proposed approach can be applied to compounds in other languages when the lexicon is available.

[5] The first line denotes a Japanese compound, the second shows word-to-word translation and the third shows translation of the compound. A mark '-' designate that forming one word by connecting with preceding morpheme.

[6] In the actual establishment, we referred to the data of technical terms mentioned in section 7. Takeuchi et al. (2001) describes in detail how to establish LCS scheme and assignment of verbs to LCSes.

to refer to specific TLCS types. Examples of deverbal nouns are also given as well in Table 1.

In Table 1, as in Figure 1, words written in capital letters (such as 'CONTROL' and 'ACT') are semantic predicates. 'x' denotes an external argument, and 'y' and 'z' denote an internal argument (see (Kageyama, 1996; Levin and Hovav, 1995)).

TLCS **1** ~ **4**, **8** and **9** represent different types of transitive verb. TLCS **11** and **12** are the types of intransitive verb. TLCS **5** represents the ergative verb and, **6**, **7** and **10** are unaccusative verbs.

The semantic predicates have combinatorial restrictions, which can be described in BNF as shown in Table 2 (⟨VERB⟩ is the root, i.e. the semantic structure of deverbal nouns).

Table 2: Restriction of TLCS predicates

⟨VERB⟩	::=	⟨BE⟩|⟨MOVE⟩|⟨BECOME⟩ |⟨CONTROL⟩|⟨ACT⟩
⟨BE⟩	::=	BE AT|NOT BE AT|BE WITH
⟨MOVE⟩	::=	MOVE TO
⟨BECOME⟩	::=	BECOME ⟨BE⟩
⟨CONTROL⟩	::=	CONTROL ⟨BE⟩|CONTROL ⟨MOVE⟩|CONTROL ⟨BECOME⟩
⟨ACT⟩	::=	ACT|ACT ON

Structures which are not listed in Table 1, such as '[CONTROL [BE WITH]]' can be derived from the rules in Table 2. It is however unlikely for them to occur in the real data.

4.1 TLCS Components

Each TLCS in Table 1 consists of the combination of semantic components that form basic meaning unit, as follows:

- 'y BE AT z' means that 'y' exists at 'z' as a state or a place.
- 'BECOME' represents that a current state changes into the next state completely. For example, '[BECOME[y BE AT z]]' means changing into the situation that 'y' exists at 'z'.
- 'y MOVE TO z' means that 'y' changes its place to 'z'.
- 'x CONTROL' means 'x' controls a predicate represented by a component that follows.
- 'x=y' represents an internal argument 'y' can change the state by itself.
- 'x ACT ON y' means the continuous action of 'x' to 'y' without changing the state of 'y'.
- 'x ACT' means the continuous action of 'x'.
- 'x BE WITH y' means that 'x' owns 'y'.
- 'NOT' represents negation.
- '[FILLED]y' means that the argument 'y' is filled with something and the verb of this TLCS cannot take an internal argument.

Table 3 shows the typology of TLCSes in relation to the TLCS components. 'Both' in Table 3 indicates that TLCS **5** have both transitive and intransitive nature[7] which is known as the transitivity alternation. Table 3 also shows the relation between traditional grammatical categories of verbs and the TLCS-based categorization of verbs.

Table 3: Typology of TLCS

argument type	TLCS num.	key compo.
transitive	1,	ACT ON
	2,3,4,8,9	CONTROL
intransitive	6,7	BECOME
	10	BE AT
	11	ACT
	12	[FILLED]y
both	5	x=y

5 Categorization of Modifier Nouns

The second lexical information necessary for the compound noun analyzer is the categorization of nouns which are to be in the modifier position of the deverbal compounds. The essential underlying assumption is this: If, as claimed in (Jackendoff, 1990; Kageyama, 1996), the LCS (and TLCS) represents a linguistically proper lexical information of verbs (including deverbal nouns) and can contribute to explaining phenomena related to the argument structure in

[7] For example, transitive case is *kaigi-o shuuryou-suru* 'meeting-ACC end-do' [end a meeting], and intransitive case is *kaigi-ga shuuryou-suru* 'meeting-NOM end-do' [a meeting ends]. Here 'ga' and 'o' designate case markers of nominative (NOM) and accusative (ACC), respectively. This phenomenon also appears in English (ex. 'break'), which is called ergative (Kageyama, 1996).

a principled way, then, correspondingly, there should be some general and principled categorization of nouns that also consistently contribute to describing phenomena related to argument structure AND this categorization can be defined vis-á-vis some basic components of the LCS scheme in a generalized and consistent manner, together with some general grammatical characteristics. Below we explain the noun categorization thus established, together with the basic features of the categorization criteria.

- **Categorization by the accusativity of modifiers**
  In Japanese compounds, there is the modifier without its accusative. This is an adjectival stem and it does not appear with inflections. Therefore, the modifier is always the adjunct in the compounds. So we introduce the distinction of '-ACC' (unaccusative) and '+ACC' (accusative).
  For example, 'kimitsu' (secrecy) and 'kioku' (memory) are '+ACC', and 'sougo' (mutual-ity) and 'kinou' (inductiv-e/ity) are '-ACC'.
- **Categorization by the basic components of TLCS**
  The basic components that contribute to the general categorization of nouns are 'ON', 'CONTROL', 'x=y' and 'BECOME [y BE AT z]'. They are used in constructing TLCS types **1**, **2**, **5** and **6**, respectively (see Table 1).
  In order to categorize nouns, we check whether they appear in sentences as an object of the verb whose TLCS has each of these specific components.
  If a noun does not appear as the object of each component, the noun is categorized as a negative category denoted by '-'. If it does, '+' is assigned. In Table 4 and in the discussion below, the categories of 'ON', 'CONTROL', 'x=y' and 'BECOME [y BE AT z]' are denoted as 'ON', 'EC(external control)', 'IC(internal control)' and 'UA(unaccusative)'. Below are examples of modifier nouns categorized as negative or positive in terms of each of these TLCS components.

ON 'koshou' (fault) and 'seinou' (performance) are '+ON', and 'heikou' (parallel) and 'rensa' (chain) are '-ON'.

EC 'imi'(semantic) and 'kairo' (circuit) are '+EC',and 'kikai' (machine) and 'densou' (transmission) are '-EC'.

IC 'fuka' (load) and 'jisoku' (flux) are '+IC', and 'kakusan' (diffusion) and 'senkei' (linearly) are '-IC'.

UA 'jiki' (magnetic) and 'joutai' (state) are '+UA', and 'junjo' (order) and 'heikou' (parallel) are '-UA'.

6 Procedure of Compound Noun Analysis

The noun categories introduced in section 5 can be used for disambiguating the intra-term relations in deverbal compounds with various deverbal heads that take different TLCS types. The range of application of the noun categorizations with respect to TLCS types is summarized in Table 4. The number in the TLCS column corresponds to the number given in Table 1.

Table 4: Categorization of combination of modifier nouns and TLCS of deverbal heads.

role	modifier category	TLCS
adjunct	-ACC	any
	-ON	1
	-EC	2,3,4
	-IC	5
	-UA	6,7
	any	10,11,12
role	modifier category	TLCS
int. argument	+ACC	8, 9
	+ON	1
	+EC	2,3,4
	+IC	5
	+UA	6,7

TLCS types **10**, **11**, and **12** do not take the internal argument relation in compounds.[8] TLCS types **8** and **9** take the internal argument relation when the modifier is '+ACC'.

Some TLCS types are formed into the groups that correspond to modifier categories in Table 4. For example, TLCS **2**,**3** and **4** form the group that corresponds to the modifier category '-EC'. This means that TLCS types in the group are regarded as the same nature from the view of the relation to the modifier category.

[8] Even though TLCS **10** has the argument 'y', we have found that the verbs in **10** always behave as ordinary nouns in compounds.

The actual analysis proceeds as follows:

Step 1 If the TLCS of the deverbal head is **10**, **11**, or **12** in Table 1, then declare the relation as adjunct and terminate. If not, go to next.

Step 2 If the modifier has the category '-ACC', then declare the relation as adjunct and terminate. If not, go to next.

Step 3 The analyzer determines the relation from the interaction of lexical meanings between a deverbal head and a modifier noun. In the case of '-ON', '-EC','-IC' or '-UA', declare the relation as adjunct and terminate. If not, go to next. It is the advantage of our approach to realize such a disambiguation based on semantic restriction.

Step 4 Declare the relation as internal argument and terminate.

With these rules and categories of nouns, we can analyze the relations between words in compounds with deverbal heads. For example, when the modifier 'kikai' (machine) is categorized as '-EC' but '+ON', the modifier in *kikai-hon'yaku* (machine-translation) is analyzed as adjunct (that means 'translation by a machine'), and the modifier in *kikai-sousa* (machine-operation) is analyzed as internal argument (that means 'operation of a machine'), both correctly.

7 Experimental Evaluation

7.1 Experiments and Results

We applied the method to 1223 two-constituent compound nouns with deverbal heads. 816 of them are taken from a dictionary of technical terms (Aiso, 1993), and 415 from news articles in a newspaper (Nikkei newspaper). In the experiment, we assumed that the compounds were segmented.

According to the manual evaluation of the experiment, 99.3% (1215 words) of the results were correct. The performance is very high. Table 5 shows the details of how the rules are applied to disambiguating the relations between constituent words in the deverbal compounds. All in all, it shows that 366 or about 30% of the disambiguation is done in Step 3 above, by referring to the relation between TLCS categories and the noun categories (while the single most frequently used category of disambiguation is '-ACC' used in step 2). This means that the method we proposed is highly important in disambiguating the intra-term relation of deverbal compounds.

Table 5: Statistics of effective rules applied to the correct analysis

process	applied rules	frequency
Step 1	in case of **10,11,12**	88
Step 2	-ACC	263
Step 3	total in step 3	366
	-ON	95
	-EC	186
	-IC	26
	-UA	59
Step 4	internal argument	498
	total	1215

7.2 Diagnosis and Discussions

We found that a small number of modifier nouns deviate from our assumptions (among the 1223 terms, we found eight). Typical cases are:

jiki	-shahei	jiki	-kioku
magnet	shield	magnet	memorize
(magnet shield)		(magnet memory)	

In the former case, the modifier is the internal argument, while in the latter it is the adjunct. The TLCS of the former deverbal head is the type **3** and that of the latter head is **2** in Table 1. The TLCS of each deverbal head is different, however, the categorization of the both TLCS types is the same according to the definition in Table 4. We categorize these TLCS types into the same group of combination rule because the TLCS **2**, **3** and **4** are a kind of causation type in Table 4. At the moment, we do not take account of the difference between TLCS **2** and **3** with the negative predicate 'NOT' because we do not have enough evidence about this. Further examination is needed to deal with cases of this type.

8 Conclusions

In this paper, we proposed a linguistic method for the analysis of compound nouns with deverbal heads. The main element of the method is the introduction of the original lexical conceptual structure, TLCS, for the deverbal nouns and the consistent categorization of the modifier nouns. Though the relations that can be disambiguated by the current framework is limited, the performance by precision is very high.

As the method is based on the linguistically clear and well-motivated perspective, the method is very promising for further extension of token coverage of the same type of phenomena as it will be easy to extend the lexicon while keeping the consistency. In addition, though not reported here, it will be possible, according to our current examination, to extend the coverage of the types of relations to be disambiguated with extensions of this framework.

Acknowledgments

We thank Prof. T. Kageyama, for giving us important suggestions on the nature of LCS. We also thank Nihonkeizashinbunsha for allowing us to use their newspaper articles (1992–1998). This work was supported in part by Japan Society for the Promotion of Science (grant no. 14780313).

References

H. Aiso. 1993. *Dictionary of Technical Terms of Information Processing (Compact edition)*. Ohmusha. (in Japanese).

K. Barker and S. Szpakowicz. 1998. Semi-Automatic Recognition of Noun Modifier Relationships. In *Proceedings of 36th Annual Meeting of the Association for Computational Linguistics*, pages 96–102.

J. Grimshaw. 1990. *Argument Structure*. MIT Press.

K. Hale and S. Keyser. 1990. *A View from the Middle Lexicon (Lexicon Project Working Papers 10)*. MIT.

J. Iida, K. Ogura, and H. Nomura. 1984. Analysis of Semantic Relations and Processing for Compound Nouns in English. In *Proceedings of Information Processing Society of Japan, SIG Notes,NL,46-4 (in Japanese)*, pages 1–8.

P. Isabelle. 1984. Another Look at Nominal Compounds. In *Proceedings of COLING-84*, pages 509–516.

R. Jackendoff. 1990. *Semantic Structures*. MIT Press.

T. Kageyama. 1996. *Verb Semantics*. Kurosio Publishers. (In Japanese).

T. Kageyama. 1999. Word Formation. In *The Handbook of Japanese Linguistics*, pages 297–325. Oxford Blackwell.

Y. Kobayasi, T. Tokunaga, and H. Tanaka. 1994. Analysis of Japanese Compound Nouns using Collocational Information. In *Proceedings of COLING-94*, pages 865–869.

M. Lauer. 1995. *Designing Statistical Language Learners: Experiments on Noun Compounds*. Ph.D. thesis, Department of Computing, Macquarie University.

Judith N. Levi. 1978. *The Syntax and Semantics of Complex Nominals*. Academic Press.

B. Levin and M. R. Hovav. 1995. *Unaccusativity*. MIT Press.

M. Rappaport and B. Levin. 1988. What to do with θ-roles. In W. Wilkins, editor, *Thematic Relations (Syntax and Semantics 21)*, pages 7–36. Academic Press.

Y. Sugioka. 1997. Projection of Arguments and Adjuncts in Compounds. In *Grant-in-Aid for COE Research Report(1) (No. 08CE1001)*, pages 185–220.

Y. Sugioka. 2000. *Transitivity Alternations in Deadjectival Verbs*. COE International Symposium at Kanda University of International Studies. http://coe-sun.kuis.ac.jp/coe/ public/paper/outside/sugioka3.pdf.

K. Takeuchi, K. Uchiyama, M. Yoshioka, K. Kageura, and T. Koyama. 2001. Categorising Deverbal Nouns Based on Lexical Conceptual Structure for Analysing Japanese Compounds. In *Proceedings of the IEEE SMC 2001 Conference*, pages 904–909.

Question Terminology and Representation for Question Type Classification

Noriko Tomuro
DePaul University
School of Computer Science, Telecommunications and Information Systems
243 S. Wabash Ave.
Chicago, IL 60604 U.S.A.
tomuro@cs.depaul.edu

Abstract

Question terminology is a set of terms which appear in keywords, idioms and fixed expressions commonly observed in questions. This paper investigates ways to automatically extract question terminology from a corpus of questions and represent them for the purpose of classifying by *question type*. Our key interest is to see whether or not semantic features can enhance the representation of strongly lexical nature of question sentences. We compare two feature sets: one with lexical features only, and another with a mixture of lexical and semantic features. For evaluation, we measure the classification accuracy made by two machine learning algorithms, C5.0 and PEBLS, by using a procedure called *domain cross-validation*, which effectively measures the *domain transferability* of features.

1 Introduction

In Information Retrieval (IR), text categorization and clustering, documents are usually indexed and represented by domain terminology: terms which are particular to the domain/topic of a document. However, when documents must be retrieved or categorized according to criteria which do not correspond to the domains, such as *genre* (text style) (Kessler et al., 1997; Finn et al., 2002) or *subjectivity* (e.g. opinion vs. factual description) (Wiebe, 2000), we must use different, domain-independent features to index and represent documents. In those tasks, selection of the features is in fact one of the most critical factors which affect the performance of a system.

Question type classification is one of such tasks, where categories are question types (e.g. 'how-to', 'why' and 'where'). In recent years, question type has been successfully used in many Question-Answering (Q&A) systems for determining the kind of entity or concept being asked and extracting an appropriate answer (Voorhees, 2000; Harabagiu et al., 2000; Hovy et al., 2001). Just like genre, question types cut across domains; for instance, we can ask 'how-to' questions in the cooking domain, the legal domain etc. However, features that constitute question types are different from those used for genre classification (typically part-of-speech or meta-lingusitic features) in that features are strongly *lexical* due to the large amount of idiosyncrasy (keywords, idioms or syntactic constructions) that is frequently observed in question sentences. For example, we can easily think of question patterns such as "What is the best way to .." and "What do I have to do to ..". In this regard, terms which identify question type are considered to form a terminology of their own, which we define as *question terminology*.

Terms in question terminology have some characteristics. First, they are mostly domain-independent, *non-content* words. Second, they include many closed-class words (such as interrogatives, modals and pronouns), and some open-class words (e.g. the noun "way" and the verb "do"). In a way, question terminology is a complement of domain terminology.

Automatic extraction of question terminology is a rather difficult task, since question terms are mixed in with content terms. Another complicating factor is paraphrasing – there are many ways to ask the same question. For example,

- "How can I clean teapots?"
- "In what way can we clean teapots?"
- "What is the best way to clean teapots?"
- "What method is used for cleaning teapots?"
- "How do I go about cleaning teapots?"

In this paper, we present the results of our investigation on how to automatically extract question terminology from a corpus of questions and represent them for the purpose of classifying by question type. It is an extension of our previous work (Tomuro and Lytinen, 2001), where we compared automatic and manual techniques to select features from questions, but only (stemmed) words were considered for features. The focus of the current work is to investigate the *kind(s)* of features, rather than selection techniques, which are best suited for representing questions for classification. Specifically, from a large dataset of questions, we automatically extracted two sets of features: one set consisting of terms (i.e., lexical features) only, and another set consisting of a mixture of terms and semantic concepts (i.e., semantic features). Our particular interest is to see whether or not semantic concepts can enhance the representation of strongly lexical nature of question sentences. To this end, we apply two machine learning algorithms (C5.0 (Quinlan, 1994) and PEBLS (Cost and Salzberg, 1993)), and compare the classification accuracy produced for the two feature sets. The results show that there is no significant increase by either algorithm by the addition of semantic features.

The original motivation behind our work on question terminology was to improve the retrieval accuracy of our system called FAQFinder (Burke et al., 1997; Lytinen and Tomuro, 2002). FAQFinder is a web-based, natural language Q&A system which uses Usenet Frequently Asked Questions (FAQ) files to answer users' questions. Figures 1 and 2 show an example session with FAQFinder. First, the user enters a question in natural language. The system then searches the FAQ files for questions that are similar to the user's. Based on the results of the search, FAQFinder displays a maximum of 5 FAQ questions which are ranked the highest by the system's similarity measure. Currently FAQFinder incorporates question type as one of the four metrics in measuring the similarity between the user's question and FAQ questions.[1] In the present implementation, the system uses a small set of manually selected words to determine the type of a question. The goal of our work here is to derive optimal features which would produce improved classification accuracy.

[1]The other three metrics are vector similarity, semantic similarity and coverage (Lytinen and Tomuro, 2002).

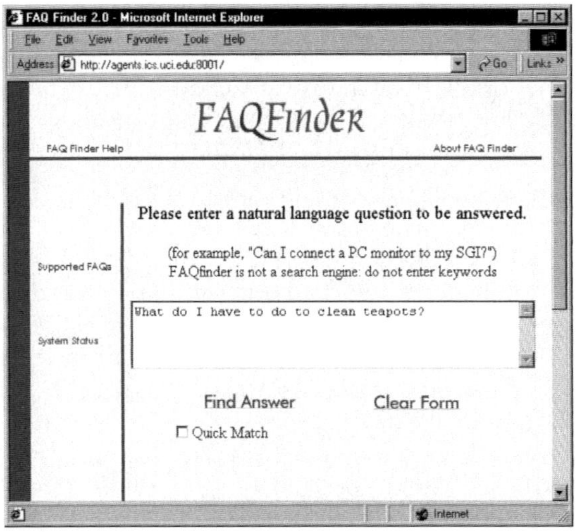

Figure 1: User question entered as a natural language query to FAQFinder

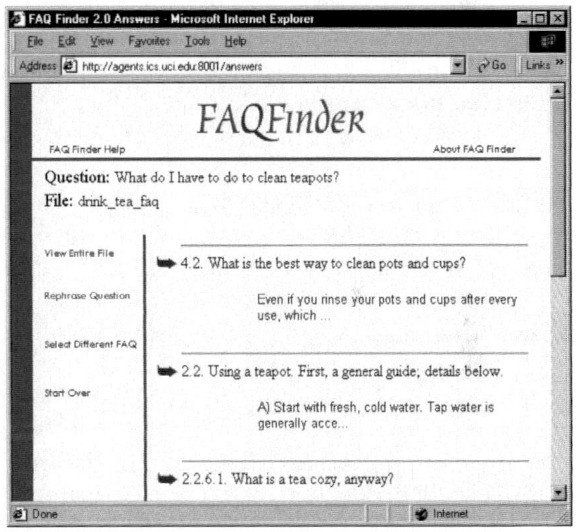

Figure 2: The 5 best-matching FAQ questions

2 Question Types

In our work, we defined 12 question types below.

1. DEF (definition)	7. PRC (procedure)
2. REF (reference)	8. MNR (manner)
3. TME (time)	9. DEG (degree)
4. LOC (location)	10. ATR (atrans)
5. ENT (entity)	11. INT (interval)
6. RSN (reason)	12. YNQ (yes-no)

Descriptive definitions of these types are found in (Tomuro and Lytinen, 2001). Table 1 shows example FAQ questions which we had used to develop the question types. Note that our question types are general question categories. They are aimed to cover a wide variety of questions entered by the FAQFinder users.

3 Selection of Feature Sets

In our current work, we utilized two feature sets: one set consisting of lexical features only (LEX), and another set consisting of a mixture of lexical features and semantic concepts (LEXSEM). Obviously, there are many known keywords, idioms and fixed expressions commonly observed in question sentences. However, categorization of some of our 12 question types seem to depend on open-class words, for instance, "What does mpg mean?" (DEF) and "What does Belgium import and export?" (REF). To distinguish those types, semantic features seem effective. Semantic features could also be useful as *back-off* features since they allow for generalization. For example, in WordNet (Miller, 1990), the noun "know-how" is encoded as a hypernym of "method", "methodology", "solution" and "technique". By selecting such abstract concepts as semantic features, we can cover a variety of paraphrases even for fixed expressions, and supplement the coverage of lexical features.

We selected the two feature sets in the following two steps. In the first step, using a dataset of 5105 example questions taken from 485 FAQ files/domains, we first manually tagged each question by question type, and then automatically derived the *initial lexical set* and *initial semantic set*. Then in the second step, we refined those initial sets by pruning irrelevant features and derived two subsets: LEX from the initial lexical set and LEXSEM from the union of lexical and semantic sets.

To evaluate various subsets tried during the selection steps, we applied two machine learning algorithms: C5.0 (the commercial version of C4.5 (Quinlan, 1994), available at `http://www.rulequest.com`), a decision tree classifier; and PEBLS (Cost and Salzberg, 1993), a k-nearest neighbor algorithm.[2] We also measured the classification accuracy by a procedure we call *domain cross-validation* (DCV). DCV is a variation of the standard cross-validation (CV) where the data is partitioned according to domains instead of random choice. To do a k-fold DCV on a set of examples from n domains, the set is first broken into k non-overlapping blocks, where each block contains examples exactly from $m = \frac{n}{k}$ domains. Then in each fold, a classifier is trained with $(k-1) * m$ domains and tested on examples from m unseen domains. Thus, by observing the classification accuracy of the target categories using DCV, we can measure the *domain transferability*: how well the features extracted from some domains transfer to other domains. Since question terminology is essentially domain-independent, DCV is a better evaluation measure than CV for our purpose.

3.1 Initial Lexical Set

The initial lexical set was obtained by ordering the words in the dataset by their *Gain Ratio* scores, then selecting the subset which produced the best classification accuracy by C5.0 and PEBLS. Gain Ratio (GR) is a metric often used in classification systems (notably in C4.5) for measuring how well a feature predicts the categories of the examples. GR is a normalized version of another metric called *Information Gain* (IG), which measures the informativeness of a feature by the number of bits required to encode the examples if they are partitioned into two sets, based on the presence or absence of the feature.[3]

Let C denote the set of categories $c_1, .., c_m$ for which the examples are classified (i.e., target categories). Given a collection of examples S, the Gain Ratio of a feature A, $GR(S, A)$, is defined as:

$$GR(S,A) = \frac{IG(S,A)}{SI(S,A)}$$

where $IG(S, A)$ is the Information Gain defined to be:

$$\begin{aligned} IG(S,A) = \; & -\textstyle\sum_{i=1}^{m} Pr(c_i)\; log_2 Pr(c_i) \\ & +Pr(A) \textstyle\sum_{i=1}^{m} Pr(c_i|A)\; log_2 Pr(c_i|A) \\ & +Pr(\overline{A}) \textstyle\sum_{i=1}^{m} Pr(c_i|\overline{A})\; log_2 Pr(c_i|\overline{A}) \end{aligned}$$

and $SI(S, A)$ is the *Splitting Information* defined to be:

$$SI(S,A) = -Pr(A)\; log_2 Pr(A) - Pr(\overline{A})\; log_2 Pr(\overline{A})$$

[2] We used k = 3 and majority voting scheme for all experiments in our current work.

[3] The description of Information Gain here is for binary partitioning. Information Gain can also be generalized to m-way partitioning, for all $m >= 2$.

Table 1: Example FAQ questions

Question Type	Question
DEF	"What does "reactivity" of emissions mean?"
REF	"What do mutual funds invest in?"
TME	"What dates are important when investing in mutual funds?"
ENT	"Who invented Octane Ratings?"
RSN	"Why does the Moon always show the same face to the Earth?"
PRC	"How can I get rid of a caffeine habit?"
MNR	"How did the solar system form?"
ATR	"Where can I get British tea in the United States?"
INT	"When will the sun die?"
YNQ	"Is the Moon moving away from the Earth?"

Then, features which yield high GR values are good predictors. In previous work in text categorization, GR (or IG) has been shown to be one of the most effective methods for reducing dimensions (i.e., words to represent each text) (Yang and Pedersen, 1997).

Here in applying GR, there was one issue we had to consider: how to distinguish content words from non-content words. This issue arose from the uneven distribution of the question types in the dataset. Since not all question types were represented in every domain, if we chose question type as the target category, features which yield high GR values might include some domain-specific words. In effect, good predictors for our purpose are words which predict question types very well, but do not predict domains. Therefore, we defined the GR score of a word to be the combination of two values: the GR value when the target category was question type, minus the GR value when the target category was domain.

We computed the (modified) GR score for 1485 words which appeared more than twice in the dataset, and applied C5.0 and PEBLS. Then we gradually reduced the set by taking the top n words according to the GR scores and observed changes in the classification accuracy. Figure 3 shows the result. The evaluation was done by using the 5-fold DCV, and the accuracy percentages indicated in the figure were an average of 3 runs. The best accuracy was achieved by the top 350 words by both algorithms; the remaining words seemed to have caused overfitting as the accuracy showed slight decline. Thus, we took the top 350 words as the initial lexical feature set.

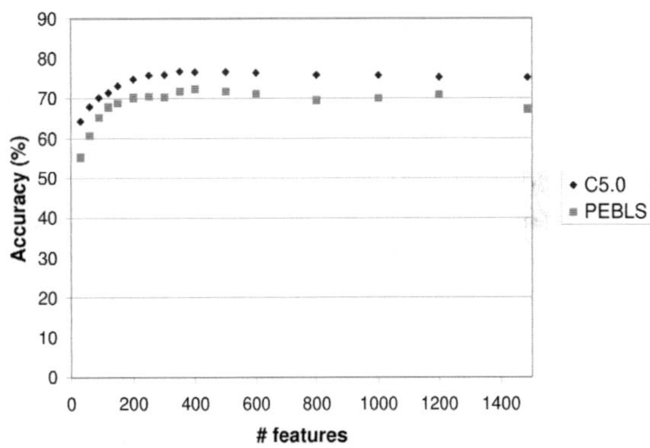

Figure 3: Classification Accuracy (%) on the training data measured by Domain Cross Validation (DCV)

3.2 Initial Semantic Set

The initial semantic set was obtained by automatically selecting some nodes in the WordNet (Miller, 1990) noun and verb trees. For each question type, we chose questions of certain structures and applied a shallow parser to extract nouns and/or verbs which appeared at a specific position. For example, for all question types (except for YNQ), we extracted the head noun from questions of the form "What is NP ..?". Those nouns are essentially the denominalization of the question type. The nouns extracted included "way", "method", "procedure", "process" for the type PRC, "reason", "advantage" for RSN, and "organization", "restaurant" for ENT. For the types DEF and MNR, we also extracted the main verb from questions of the form "How/What does NP V ..?". Such verbs included "work", "mean" for DEF, and "affect" and "form" for MNR.

Then for the nouns and verbs extracted for each question type, we applied the sense disambiguation algorithm used in (Resnik, 1997) and derived semantic classes (or nodes in the WordNet trees) which were their abstract generalization. For each word in a set, we traversed the WordNet tree upward through the hypernym links from the nodes which corresponded to the first two senses of the word, and assigned each ancestor a value which equaled to the inverse of the distance (i.e., the number of links traversed) from the original node. Then we accumulated the values for all ancestors, and selected ones (excluding the top nodes) whose value was above a threshold. For example, the set of nouns extracted for the type PRC were "know-how" (an ancestor of "way" and "method") and "activity" (an ancestor of "procedure" and "process").

By applying the procedure above for all question types, we obtained a total of 112 semantic classes. This constitutes the initial semantic set.

3.3 Refinement

The final feature sets, LEX and LEXSEM, were derived by further refining the initial sets. The main purpose of refinement was to reduce the union of initial lexical and semantic sets (a total of 350 + 112 = 462 features) and derive LEXSEM. It was done by taking the features which appeared in more than half of the decision trees induced by C5.0 during the iterations of DCV.[4] Then we applied the same procedure to the initial lexical set (350 features) and derived LEX. Now both sets were (sub) optimal subsets, with which we could make a fair comparison. There were 117 features/words and 164 features selected for LEX and LEXSEM respectively.

Our refinement method is similar to (Cardie, 1993) in that it selects features by removing ones that did not appear in a decision tree. The difference is that, in our method, each decision tree is induced from a strict subset of the domains of the dataset. Therefore, by taking the intersection of multiple such trees, we can effectively extract features that are domain-independent, thus transferable to other unseen domains. Our method is also computationally less expensive and feasible, given the number of features expected to be in the reduced set (over a hundred by our intuition), than other feature subset selection techniques, most of which require expensive search through model space (such as *wrapper* approach (John et al., 1994)).

Table 2: Classification accuracy (%) on the training set by using reduced feature sets

Feature set	# features	C5.0	PEBLS
Initial lex	350	76.7	71.8
LEX (reduced)	117	77.4	74.5
Initial lex + sem	462	76.7	71.8
LEXSEM (reduced)	164	77.7	74.7

Table 2 shows the classification accuracy measured by DCV for the training set. The increase of the accuracy after the refinement was minimal using C5.0 (from 76.7 to 77.4 for LEX, from 76.7 to 77.7 for LEXSEM), as expected. But the increase using PEBLS was rather significant (from 71.8 to 74.5 for LEX, from 71.8 to 74.7 for LEXSEM). This result agreed with the findings in (Cardie, 1993), and confirmed that LEX and LEXSEM were indeed (sub) optimal. However, the difference between LEX and LEXSEM was not statistically significant by either algorithm (from 77.4 to 77.7 by C5.0, from 74.5 to 74.7 by PEBLS; p-values were .23 and .41 respectively[5]). This means the semantic features did not help improve the classification accuracy.

As we inspected the results, we discovered that, out of the 164 features in LEXSEM, 32 were semantic features, and they did occur in 33% of the training examples ($1671/5105 \approx .33$). However in most of those examples, key terms were already represented by lexical features, thus semantic features did not add any more information to help determine the question type. As an example, a sentence "What are the dates of the upcoming Jewish holidays?" was represented by lexical features "what", "be", "of" and "date", and a semantic feature "time-unit" (an ancestor of "date").

The 117 words in LEX are listed in the Appendix at the end of this paper.

[4]We have in fact experimented various threshold values. It turned out that .5 produced the best accuracy.

[5]P-values were obtained by applying the t-test on the accuracy produced by all iterations of DCV, with a null hypothesis that the mean accuracy of LEXSEM was higher than that of LEX.

Table 3: Classification accuracy (%) on the testsets

Feature set	# features	FAQFinder		AskJeeves	
		C5.0	PEBLS	C5.0	PEBLS
LEX	117	67.8	66.6	77.3	73.9
LEXSEM	164	67.5	67.1	73.7	71.1

3.4 External Testsets

To further investigate the effect of semantic features, we tested LEX and LEXSEM with two external testsets: one set consisting of 620 questions taken from FAQFinder user log, and another set consisting of 3485 questions taken from the AskJeeves (`http://www.askjeeves.com`) user log. Both datasets contained questions from a wide range of domains, therefore served as an excellent indicator of the domain transferability for our two feature sets.

Table 3 shows the results. For the FAQFinder data, LEX and LEXSEM produced comparable accuracy using both C5.0 and PEBLS. But for the AskJeeves data, LEXSEM did worse than LEX consistently by both classifiers. This means the additional semantic features were interacting with lexical features.

We speculate the reason to be the following. Compared to the FAQFinder data, the AskJeeves data was gathered from a much wider audience, and the questions spanned a broad range of domains. Many terms in the questions were from vocabulary considerably larger than that of our training set. Therefore, the data contained quite a few words whose hypernym links lead to a semantic feature in LEXSEM but did not fall into the question type keyed by the feature. For instance, a question in AskJeeves "What does Hanukah mean?" was mis-classified as type TME by using LEXSEM. This was because "Hanukah" in WordNet was encoded as a hyponym of "time_period". On the other hand, LEX did not include "Hanukah", thus correctly classified the question as type DEF.

4 Related Work

Recently, with a need to incorporate user preferences in information retrieval, several work has been done which classifies documents by genre. For instance, (Finn et al., 2002) used machine learning techniques to identify subjective (opinion) documents from newspaper articles. To determine what feature adapts well to unseen domains, they compared three kinds of features: words, part-of-speech statistics and manually selected meta-linguistic features. They concluded that the part-of-speech performed the best with regard to domain transfer. However, not only were their feature sets pre-determined, their features were distinct from words in the documents (or features were the entire words themselves), thus no feature subset selection was performed.

(Wiebe, 2000) also used machine learning techniques to identify subjective sentences. She focused on adjectives as an indicator of subjectivity, and used corpus statistics and lexical semantic information to derive adjectives that yielded high precision.

5 Conclusions and Future Work

In this paper, we showed that semantic features did not enhance lexical features in the representation of questions for the purpose of question type classification. While semantic features allow for generalization, they also seemed to do more harm than good in some cases by interacting with lexical features. This indicates that question terminology is strongly lexical indeed, and suggests that enumeration of words which appear in typical, idiomatic question phrases would be more effective than semantics.

For future work, we are planning to experiment with synonyms. The use of synonyms is another way of increasing the coverage of question terminology; while semantic features try to achieve it by generalization, synonyms do it by lexical expansion. Our plan is to use the synonyms obtained from very large corpora reported in (Lin, 1998). We are also planning to compare the (lexical and semantic) features we derived automatically in this work with manually selected features. In our previous work, manually selected (lexical) features showed slightly better performance for the training data but no significant difference for the test data. We plan to manually pick out semantic as well as lexical features, and apply to the current data.

References

R. Burke, K. Hammond, V. Kulyukin, S. Lytinen, N. Tomuro, and S. Schoenberg. 1997. Question answering from frequently asked question files: Experiences with the faqfinder system. *AI Magazine*, 18(2).

C. Cardie. 1993. Using decision trees to improve case-based learning. In *Proceedings of the 10th International Conference on Machine Learning (ICML-93)*.

S. Cost and S. Salzberg. 1993. A weighted nearest neighbor algorithm for learning with symbolic features. *Machine Learning*, 10(1).

A. Finn, N. Kushmerick, and B. Smyth. 2002. Genre classification and domain transfer for information filtering. In *Proceedings of the European Colloquium on Information Retrieval Research*, Glasgow.

S. Harabagiu, D. Moldovan, M. Pasca, R. Mihalcea, M. Surdeanu, R. Bunescu, R. Girju, V. Rus, and P. Morarescu. 2000. Falcon: Boosting knowledge for answer engines. In *Proceedings of TREC-9*.

E. Hovy, L. Gerber, U. Hermjakob, C. Lin, and D. Ravichandran. 2001. Toward semantics-based answer pinpointing. In *Proceedings of the DARPA Human Language Technologies (HLT)*.

G. John, R. Kohavi, and K. Pfleger. 1994. Irrelevant features and the subset selection problem. In *Proceedings of the 11th International Conference on Machine Learning (ICML-94)*.

K. Kessler, G. Nunberg, and H. Schutze. 1997. Automatic detection of text genre. In *Proceedings of the 35th Annual Meeting of the Association for Computational Linguistics (ACL-97)*.

D. Lin. 1998. Automatic retrieval and clustering of similar words. In *Proceedings of the 36th Annual Meeting of the Association for Computational Linguistics (ACL-98)*.

S. Lytinen and N. Tomuro. 2002. The use of question types to match questions in faqfinder. In *Papers from the 2002 AAAI Spring Symposium on Mining Answers from Texts and Knowledge Bases*.

G. Miller. 1990. Wordnet: An online lexical database. *International Journal of Lexicography*, 3(4).

R. Quinlan. 1994. *C4.5: Programs for Machine Learning*. Morgan Kaufman.

P. Resnik. 1997. Selectional preference and sense disambiguation. In *Proceedings of the ACL SIGLEX Workshop on Tagging Text with Lexical Semantics*, Washington D.C.

N. Tomuro and S. Lytinen. 2001. Selecting features for paraphrasing question sentences. In *Proceedings of the workshop on Automatic Paraphrasing at NLP Pacific Rim 2001 (NLPRS-2001)*, Tokyo, Japan.

E. Voorhees. 2000. The trec-9 question answering track report. In *Proceedings of TREC-9*.

J. Wiebe. 2000. Learning subjective adjectives from corpora. In *Proceedings of the 17th National Conference on Artificial Intelligence (AAAI-2000)*, Austin, Texas.

Y. Yang and J. Pedersen. 1997. A comparative study on feature selection in text categorization. In *Proceedings of the 14th International Conference on Machine Learning (ICML-97)*.

Appendix: The LEX Set

"about" "address" "advantage" "affect" "and" "any" "archive" "available" "bag" "be" "begin" "benefit" "better" "buy" "can" "cause" "clean" "come" "company" "compare" "contact" "contagious" "copy" "cost" "create" "date" "day" "deal" "differ" "difference" "do" "effect" "emission" "evaporative" "expense" "fast" "find" "for" "get" "go" "good" "handle" "happen" "have" "history" "how" "if" "in" "internet" "keep" "know" "learn" "long" "make" "many" "mean" "milk" "much" "my" "name" "number" "obtain" "of" "often" "old" "on" "one" "or" "organization" "origin" "people" "percentage" "place" "planet" "price" "procedure" "pronounce" "purpose" "reason" "relate" "relationship" "shall" "shuttle" "site" "size" "sky" "so" "solar" "some" "start" "store" "sun" "symptom" "take" "tank" "tax" "that" "there" "time" "to" "us" "way" "web" "what" "when" "where" "which" "who" "why" "will" "with" "work" "world_wide_web" "wrong" "www" "year" "you"

Acquisition of Lexical Paraphrases from Texts

Kazuhide Yamamoto
ATR Spoken Language Translation Research Laboratories
2-2-2, Hikaridai, Seika-cho, Soraku-gun, Kyoto, 619-0288 Japan
yamamoto@fw.ipsj.or.jp

Abstract

Automatic acquisition of paraphrase knowledge for content words is proposed. Using only a non-parallel text corpus, we compute the paraphrasability metrics between two words from their similarity in context. We then filter words such as proper nouns from external knowledge. Finally, we use a heuristic in further filtering to improve the accuracy of the automatic acquisition. In this paper, we report the results of acquisition experiments.

1 Introduction

Paraphrasing research has attracted increased attention, and the work in this field has become more active recently. Paraphrasing involves various types of transformations of expressions into the same language, and thus there is generally no all-purpose design and information resource. Among the many types of paraphrasing, a handwritten construction may be best for syntactic paraphrasing knowledge or knowledge of functional words because the number of resulting phenomena can be counted. On the other hand, we need to acquire lexical paraphrasing knowledge automatically or efficiently, since there is an enormous number of phenomena observed for an enormous number of content words.

Some works, such as Barzilay and McKeown (2001), have acquired paraphrasing knowledge automatically. All of those works found differences from a *paraphrase corpus*, where each expression is aligned to another expression (or more) with the same meaning and in the same language. Unfortunately, there is no paraphrase corpus widely available except for a few collections such as those prepared by Shirai et al. (2001) and Zhang et al. (2001). Most of those works collected paraphrase corpora by employing special situations, such as multiple news resources from the same events or multiple translations of the same (and well-known) story in other languages. However, since these situations seem to be really special, we believe that the collection of many paraphrase corpora in the near future is quite hopeless. Consequently, it is necessary to conduct a feasibility study on collecting various kinds of paraphrase knowledge from non-paraphrase corpora, particularly from raw text corpora. Although we have already reported extracting paraphrasing knowledge of Japanese noun modifiers from a raw corpus (Kataoka et al., 1999), we need to explore other types of expressions.

With this motivation, we have attempted to acquire paraphrasing knowledge on content words, mainly nouns and verbs. As a knowledge source, we use newspaper articles collected over one year in text format, which is regarded as the most generally used corpus. In this trial, we propose the following two principles of acquisition:

- Conditions for applying each type of paraphrasing knowledge should be obtained.
- Paraphrasing knowledge should have directionality.

In other words, all of the paraphrasing patterns obtained by the conventional methods seem to have been applied unconditionally, that is, conventional approaches tend to target only unconditional patterns. However, most paraphrasing phenomena depend on their context; paraphrasing can be possible only if a paraphrased expression fits the context.

Moreover, directionality of the rules is an important issue for paraphrasing, although no other works have discussed this. Despite the existence of synonymy, even if expression E_1 can be replaced by expression E_2, it is unsure whether E_2 can be paraphrased by using E_1. We discuss this feature in the experiments.

2 Contextual Similarity vs. Synonymy

Paraphrasability is the degree of replacability for two expressions E_1 and E_2, which are regarded as different from each other in some sense. This definition implies the notion that E_1 should not be judged as the same (or similar) as E_2 in the sense of meaning. Of course, similarity of meaning and paraphrasability are very closely correlated with each other, and Kurohashi and Sakai (1999) utilize this feature to paraphrase Japanese expressions (in order to comprehend them more easily). They use a Japanese dictionary written for humans (or more precisely, children) to replace a part of the target expression with a different one by judging its local context computed by a thesaurus.

We propose that replacability (obtained by the corpus, for example) is a more important factor in judging the paraphrasability of expressions than their meaning as defined in a dictionary. For example, words used only in some special situations, such as for children or in ancient documents, should not be used in a paraphrase even though it has synonymy.

On the contrary, even if synonymy is not satisfied, we still focus on expressions that are replaceable. Hypernymy is one example of this. A hypernym is not a paraphrase in a strict sense due to the loss of information. However, this kind of paraphrasing is still useful from the engineering point of view. For instance, these *loose* (and therefore many) paraphrases are more effective in the case of reluctant processing, where we must necessarily change an expression for various reasons such as our requirement in paraphrase-based machine translation (Yamamoto, 2002). Moreover, this kind of paraphrase loses nothing when it is used as anaphora or when it is trivial and out of major interest in the context used. Not all hypernyms are always paraphrasable, so we cannot list this type of paraphrase from only a thesaurus.

3 Approach and Implementation

This section describes our approach to acquiring paraphrase knowledge from a text corpus. We use Perl programming language to implement all of the following processes and experiments.

3.1 Collection of context from corpus

We first define the term *context* in this paper. The context of a certain content word is defined as direct dependency relations between the word and the words that surround it in texts. That is, the context of a content word c is, in our sense, defined as the collection of words upon which c directly depends as well as the collection of words that directly depend on c.

Under this definition, we first collected all of the dependency relations observed in the corpus. Each article is segmented and part-of-speech tagged by the morphological analyzer JUMAN[1] and then parsed by the KNP[2] parser. We then obtained a relation triplet (c_1, r, c_2) from each article, where a word c_1 depends on a word c_2 with the relation r. A complete list of r types and their examples is shown below:

- (Noun, r_1, Noun)
  e.g. '今度 (this time) の (of) 法律 (law)'
  'テロ (terrorism) 法案 (bill)'
- (Adjective, r_2, Noun)
  e.g. '新たな (new) 法律 (law)'
- (Noun, r_3, Verb)
  e.g. '衆議院 (Lower House) が (SUB) 可決する (approve)'
- (Verb, r_4, Noun)
  e.g. '空爆する (bombing) 米軍 (U.S. army)'

In this list, r_i can be a particle, such as a case particle (r_3) or an associative particle "の" (r_1). Another type of possible r_i in the list is a syntactic relation expressed without any particle or other functional marker. For instance, a verb or an adjective directly modifies a noun without using any functional words in Japanese. In this case, we introduce the notion of a constituent boundary proposed by Furuse and Iida

[1] http://www-nagao.kuee.kyoto-u.ac.jp/nl-resource/juman-e.html

[2] http://www-nagao.kuee.kyoto-u.ac.jp/nl-resource/knp-e.html

(1994), which is a virtual functional marker inserted between two consecutive content words, in order to more easily analyze a sentence. For instance, if there are two consecutive nouns, we assume that $\langle nn \rangle$ is inserted between the two nouns, and consequently the relation r_i is $\langle nn \rangle$.

3.2 Bigraph construction

We then transform the collection of triplets into a bigraph (2-partite graph). In the first step, each triplet in the collection is converted into two couplets consisting of a content word and an operator by the following definition: an operator consists of a content word c and a relation with directionality r. It is defined as either $r \rightarrow c$ (something depends on c by r) or $r \leftarrow c$ (c depends on something by r). For instance, suppose that a triplet is (c_1, r, c_2), then both a couplet for the first content word c_1, i.e., (c_1, $r \rightarrow c_2$) and a couplet for the second content word c_2, i.e., (c_2, $r \leftarrow c_1$) are extracted in this operation.

We perform this conversion for all of the triplets, and a list of couplets is obtained. From the viewpoint of graph theory, this couplet list is a bigraph, such as figure 1, which consists of two sets (content word set and operator set) and a list of edges, where each edge connects an element in one set to an element on the other side. This bigraph is a weighted graph, and each weight expresses the frequency of appearing in the corpus.

3.3 Paraphrasability computation

In the next step, we compute paraphrasability. In this work, the paraphrasability P for any two content words c_i and c_j is defined in the following formula:

$$P(c_i, c_j) = \frac{\sum_{m \in M(c_i) \cap M(c_j)} p(m, c_i)}{\sum_{m \in M(c_i)} p(m, c_i)} \quad (1)$$

$$M(c_i) = \{m | f(m, c_i) > 1\} \quad (2)$$

$$p(m, c_i) = \frac{f(m, c_i)}{\sum_c f(m, c)} \quad (3)$$

In this formula, let $f(m_0, c_0)$ be frequency of content word c_0 with operator m_0. In other words, $f(m_0, c_0)$ is a weight of edge (c_0, m_0) in the bigraph.

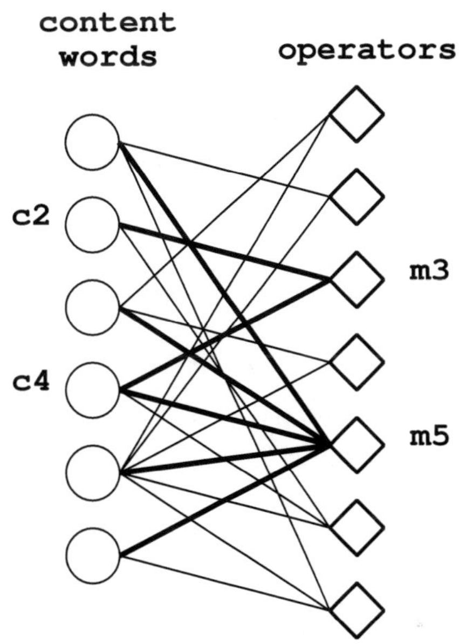

Figure 1: Example of a bigraph (2-partite graph)

This formulation can be explained as follows. Paraphrasability between two content words c_i and c_j increases if these words behave similarly in terms of their dependency relations. That is, this metrics compares the similarity of the contextual situations of the two input words. The definition states that paraphrasability computes the number of operators that c_j links among the operators that c_i links.

However, we believe that the importance of each operator m is not equivalent to that of the others. For example, in figure 1, the operator m_3 is linked by only two words, c_2 and c_4, while the operator m_5 is linked by almost all of the words. In this situation, it is not reasonable to handle the two operators equally, since m_3 may confirm that the two words are similar or paraphrasable, whereas m_5 may be a general operator widely used in various situations. In other words, when we compute paraphrasability from c_2 to c_4, the edge (c_4, m_5) is judged as less important than the edge (c_4, m_3) or (c_2, m_3). Consequently, each operator is weighted by the definition of formula (3). Moreover, instances of low frequency are regarded as accidental and insignificant, so we filter out links where an instance appears only once.

It is obvious in the definition of (1) that $0 \leq P(c_i, c_j) \leq 1$, and a higher score expresses a higher possibility of paraphrasing. More importantly, the definition indicates the relation $P(c_i, c_j) \neq P(c_j, c_i)$, i.e., there is a directionality that gives larger differences than any similarity metrics. Even if an expression E_1 has a large paraphrasability for an expression E_2, it is completely uncertain whether the paraphrasability of E_2 into E_1 is high or low.

3.4 Paraphrase knowledge filtering

By only taking the discussion of the last subsection into account, we can compute paraphrasability between any two content words. However, this measure is not the final judgment of paraphrasability: some pairs score very high even though they are not paraphrasable. For example, the pair *three* and *four* may have a very high score but are of course not paraphrasable. In our observation, the following kinds are found to be misjudged as paraphrasable by our definitions.

1. number, e.g., '三'(three) →'四'(four)
2. proper noun, e.g., '北京'(Beijing) →'台北'(Taipei)
3. antonym, e.g., '右'(right) →'左'(left)

Obviously, these errors occurred due to one of the limitations of our approach; since the formula only has an interest in the context of the words found in the corpus, not in the sense of the words found in a dictionary.

However, we can filter out these kinds of word pairs by introducing language resources external to the corpus. First, we can judge whether the word is a number by applying some simple rules. Second, we can now easily obtain extensive lists of both major proper nouns and antonyms. We obtain the proper noun list from GoiTaikei[3], one of the largest Japanese electronic thesauri, in which 169,682 proper noun entries are extracted. We obtain the antonym list from both Gakken Kokugo Daijiten (a Japanese word dictionary) and Kadokawa Ruigo Shinjiten (a Japanese thesaurus), which have 11,981 antonym pairs in total.

[3]http://www.kecl.ntt.co.jp/icl/mtg/resources/GoiTaikei/

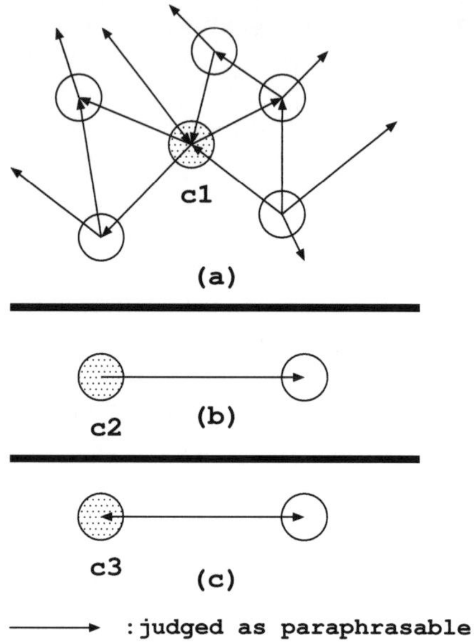

Figure 2: Heuristic by number of links

In fact, further filtering is necessary in order to reduce errors. For example, in English, *guitar*, *piano*, and *flute* have very similar contexts, such as "*to play the* _____," "*an electric* _____," "*a violin and a* _____," and so on, although they are naturally not paraphrasable. We predict that in order to use lexical paraphrase collection for filtering, future research will need to concentrate on how to collect word pairs that are not paraphrasable but have the same context.

3.5 Further filtering by heuristic method

In the final process, we filter the pairs further by using our proposed heuristic to improve the acquisition accuracy.

From our observations of the results obtained by the above operations, we found a clear tendency in words that have a very high frequency or very broad sense: these words tend to be judged as having a high paraphrasability from many words or to many words, even if they are not actually paraphrasable. For example, in figure 2 (a), a content word such as c_1 tends to be misjudged as paraphrasable if c_1 links to many words and/or if c_1 is linked by many words. In other words, case (b) of the figure, where a word c_2 connects to only one word, would more likely have its paraphrasing judged as proper. We also build a hypothesis that case (c), where

Table 1: Evaluation for Content Words

	Case 1	Case 2	Total
Extracted	668	1149	1684
Paraphrasable	422	780	1117
Accuracy	63.2%	67.9%	66.3%

Case 1: a word paraphrases to one word
Case 2: a word is paraphrased from one word

two words are exchangeable, has more accuracy than the other two cases, which are evaluated in the next section.

We assume these errors occurred because such words can have dependency relations with many words, i.e., such words are general and frequently appearing. Consequently, such cases are unexpectedly judged as being highly paraphrasable from or to many words. As these words are used many times in many contexts, the possibility of inserted noises also increases. Therefore, distinguishing noises from real paraphrases becomes difficult.

These spurious paraphrases should not remain in the final results, so we conduct another filtering according to the above analysis. The actual process is conducted as follows. For each c_i, we count the number of c_j that satisfies the relation $P(c_i, c_j) > P_{const}$. If there is only one word c_j that satisfies this relation, we finally determine that c_i can paraphrase to c_j. Similarly, for each c_j, we count the number of c_i that satisfies the relation $P(c_i, c_j) > P_{const}$. If there is only one word c_i that satisfies the relation, we finally determine that c_i can paraphrase to c_j. In the experiment below, we set $P_{const} = 0.1$.

In this heuristic filtering, some word pairs that are actually paraphrasable may, unfortunately, also be lost. The problem of saving them remains for our future work.

4 Knowledge Acquisition Experiment

4.1 Experiment on content word paraphrasing

We have conducted an experiment of paraphrasing knowledge acquisition in the following conditions. The corpus we used was all articles of The Mainichi Shimbun, which is one of the national daily newspapers of Japan, published in the year 1995. The size of the corpus is 87.3 MB, consisting of 1.33 million sentences.

[4]These two words have the same string but different part-of-speech, so our tagger judges these two as different.

Table 2: Highest Paraphrasable Pairs

Paraphrase pair	P	P (←)
逸話 (anecdote) → 話 (story)	1	.0015
したてなげ → うわてなげ	1	.2539*
かぎり (only) → 限り (only)	1	.1877*
図式 (scheme) → 構図 (form)	.9982	.2671*
パニック (panic) → 混乱 (confusion)	.9978	.0496
勝ち (win) → 勝ち (win)[4]	.9802	.5176*
ホッケー (hockey) → 野球 (baseball)	.9752	.0286
結党 (formation) → 結成 (formation)	.9672	.0449
違和感 (incongruity) → 痛み (pain)	.9667	.0352
激変 (drastic change) → 変化 (change)	.9582	.0177

Table 1 illustrates evaluation results of knowledge acquisition. The results show that our proposed process can choose approximately 1,700 paraphrase pairs that have 66% accuracy. Although this accuracy is not satisfactory for an automatic process, it is already helpful from the engineering point of view; accordingly, we can obtain a large amount of high-quality paraphrase pairs with a minimum human check in significantly less time than one day.

We also show the acquired paraphrase pairs with the highest paraphrasabilities in Table 2. Note that P (←) in the table denotes the paraphrasability of the inverted paraphrases, from right to left direction, and the symbol * indicates that this direction is also judged as paraphrasable, i.e., these two words are determined to be paraphrasable with each other. We found that most of the entries in the list are correctly judged to be paraphrasable, even though some of them cannot be paraphrasable, such as "したてなげ (underarm throwing)" into "うわてなげ (overarm throwing)"[5].

We can also confirm that the directionality of the proposed measure works quite well. For example, we can paraphrase the term "逸話 (anecdote)" with the more general term "話 (story)," but it is impossible to replace the latter with the former except in some restricted context. The outputs seen in this table illustrate such an intuition.

[5]Both are names of techniques in *sumo* wrestling.

Table 3: Paraphrasability of Operators

Paraphrase pair	P
依頼 (request) が → 注文 (order) が	1
理事 (director) を → 教授 (professor) を	.9940
支部 (branch) で → 地裁 (district court) で	.9334
高裁 (high court) で → 地裁 で	.8734
$\langle nn\rangle$ 短期 (short term) →$\langle nn\rangle$ 短大 (college)	.8723
$\langle nn\rangle$ ヤ (Swallows) →$\langle nn\rangle$ 巨 (Giants)	.8553
毎週 (every week) $\langle nn\rangle$→$\langle nn\rangle$ 夜 (night)	.8123
市議 (city councillor) $\langle nn\rangle$→ 県議 $\langle nn\rangle$	.8063
十数 (several) $\langle nn\rangle$→ 数 (several) $\langle nn\rangle$	.7961
県議 (pref. assemblyman) $\langle nn\rangle$→ 市議 $\langle nn\rangle$	.7859

If the process judges that the two words can paraphrase each other, these words are considered to be a paraphrase in a narrow sense. In this experiment, we can extract 114 pairs that satisfy this relation, and 75 of these pairs are evaluated as being correct, for an accuracy of 65.8%.

4.2 Experiment for acquisition of operator paraphrase

So far in this paper, we have been using an operator set to compute any of two words in the content word set in the bigraph. We found that we can also do this in the reverse way: computing any of two operators by using the content word set. This is possible because even if we turn a bigraph upside-down, it is still a bigraph. In this subsection, we report an experiment on computing the paraphrasability of operators by the same procedure as above.

After multiple filtering, 432 pairs were judged as paraphrasable. From these we found that the number of correct pairs was 312 (72.2% accuracy). Table 3 illustrates the final paraphrasable pairs with the highest paraphrasability.

Unfortunately, these pairs include errors, so their performance in an automatic process should be improved. However, this performance is still promising for a human-assisted tool.

We investigated the pairs and found that there were various kinds of paraphrasing knowledge obtained in this process. Not only paraphrases of content words but also paraphrase knowledge of the following types were obtained in this experiment.

- insertion and deletion of the particle "の" in noun-noun sequences
- paraphrasing for case particles; in Japanese, it may be possible to change a particle under a certain context.
- voice conversion
- different description of the same word, e.g., from a Chinese-origin word to a native Japanese word

5 Related Works

Lexical paraphrasing is very useful in information retrieval, since it is necessary to expand terms for improving retrieval coverage. Jacquemin et al. (1997) have proposed acquiring syntactic and morpho-syntactic variations of the multi-word terms using a corpus-based approach. They have searched for variation, i.e., similar expressions using (a part of) the input words, such as *technique for measurement* against *measurement technique*, while our target is the paraphrase of a single content word.

The goal of our work is to obtain lexical knowledge for paraphrasing. For this purpose we use contextual similarity, which is also used in the sense similarity computation task in the fields of natural language processing, artificial intelligence, and cognitive science. Moreover, the idea of corpus-based context extraction is basically the same and also used in the task of automatic construction of thesauri or sense determination of unknown words.

Although this is the first work to use context for paraphrase knowledge extraction, many previously reported works have used context for similarity calculation. Paraphrasability and word sense similarity may seem like similar metrics, but there are critical differences between the two tasks. First, similarity satisfies the symmetrical property while paraphrasability does not (explained in 3.3). Second, similarity is a relative measure while paraphrasability is an absolute measure; in many cases, we can answer "*Can E_1 paraphrase to E_2?*", but it is hard to answer "*Is E_1 similar to E_2?*". In other words, it is important to collect paraphrases while it may be pointless to collect *similar words*, since the border for the former is clearer than that of the latter.

The kind of information used for defining context is important. For this question, Nagamatsu and Tanaka (1996) used a deep case (seen in a semantically tagged corpus), and Kanzaki et al. (2000) only extracted relations of nominal modification. The most closely related work in terms of similarity source is the work of Grefenstette (1994), where they obtained subject-verb, verb-object, adjective-noun, and noun-noun relations from a corpus. In contrast, as discussed in subsection 3.1, we propose extracting all of the dependency relations around content words, i.e., nouns, verbs, and adjectives. This is the first attempt to introduce these features into a context definition, and it is obvious that coverage of extracted pairs becomes wider by using various features. However, we have not conducted enough experiments to prove that these factors are effective. This remains for our future work.

6 Conclusions

We propose a process to acquire paraphrasing pairs of content words from a non-parallel raw corpus. We utilize contextual similarity, obtained from the corpus, to compute paraphrasability between any two content words. Some of the word pairs that unexpectedly have high paraphrasability are filtered out by using external linguistic knowledge such as proper nouns and antonyms. Moreover, our proposed heuristic, obtained through observation, can increase acquisition accuracy. These processes in combination are able to obtain more than 1,700 paraphrase pairs with approximately 66% accuracy.

Our interest in this research is not to pursue higher accuracy in automatic processing but to obtain any kind of paraphrasing knowledge as fast as possible. From this point of view, the coverage of the acquisition process is a more serious problem for us than accuracy. Our preliminary experiment showed that a drastic drop in accuracy is observed even if we increase coverage gradually. We need to find another filtering criterion to avoid this problem.

Acknowledgment

The research reported here was supported in part by a contract with the Telecommunications Advancement Organization of Japan entitled, "A study of speech dialogue translation technology based on a large corpus."

References

Regina Barzilay and Kathleen R. McKeown. 2001. Extracting paraphrases from a parallel corpus. In *Proc. of ACL-2001*, pages 50–57.

Osamu Furuse and Hitoshi Iida. 1994. Constituent boundary parsing for example-based machine translation. In *Proc. of Coling'94*, pages 105–111.

Gregory Grefenstette. 1994. Corpus-derived first, second, third-order word affinities. In *Proc. of EURALEX'94*.

Christian Jacquemin, Judith L. Klavans, and Evelyne Tzoukermann. 1997. Expansion of multi-word terms for indexing and retrieval using morphology and syntax. In *Proc. of ACL-EACL'97*, pages 24–31.

Kyoto Kanzaki, Qing Ma, and Hitoshi Isahara. 2000. Similarities and differences among semantic behaviors of Japanese adnominal constituents. In *Proc. of ANLP/NAACL 2000 Workshop on Syntactic and Semantic Complexity in Natural Language Processing System*, pages 59–68.

Akira Kataoka, Shigeru Masuyama, and Kazuhide Yamamoto. 1999. Summarization by shortening a Japanese noun modifier into expression "A no B". In *Proc. of NLPRS'99*, pages 409–414.

Sadao Kurohashi and Yasuyuki Sakai. 1999. Semantic analysis of Japanese noun phrases: A new approach to dictionary-based understanding. In *Proc. of ACL'99*, pages 481–488.

Kenji Nagamatsu and Hidehiko Tanaka. 1996. Estimating point-of-view-based similarity using POV reinforcement and similarity propagation. In *Proc. of Pacific Asia Conference on Language, Information, and Computation (PACLIC)*, pages 373–382.

Satoshi Shirai, Kazuhide Yamamoto, and Francis Bond. 2001. Japanese-English paraphrase corpus. In *Proc. of NLPRS2001 Workshop on Language Resources in Asia*, pages 23–30.

Kazuhide Yamamoto. 2002. Machine translation by interaction between paraphraser and transfer. In *Proc. of COLING2002*.

Yujie Zhang, Kazuhide Yamamoto, and Masashi Sakamoto. 2001. Paraphrasing utterances by reordering words using semi-automatically acquired patterns. In *Proc. of NLPRS2001*, pages 195–202.